THE RISE OF THE GREAT SOUTHERN LAND

THE REPUBLIC OF AUSTRALIA 2023

DAVID SHAUN LARSEN

Copyright © 2017, by David Shaun Larsen

www.davidshaunlarsen.com

The opinions and suggestions expressed in this book are purely the author's own and do not necessarily reflect the official policy or position of any other agency, organisation, employer or company (unless directly referenced by a Government funded body whose role is to provide information and services for the community).

It is the reader's responsibility to verify their own facts.

No part of this book may be reproduced in any form or by any electronic or mechanical means, including information storage and retrieval systems, without written permission from the author, except for the use of brief quotations in a book review.

Requests to publish any work from this book can be emailed to:

davidsdm@yahoo.com

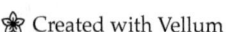

CONTENTS

Acknowledgments   v
Introduction   vii

1. Australian Indigenous Culture   1
2. Politics for Our Age   19
3. The Republic of Australia   34
4. Challenges for Humanity   45
5. Gender Equality   54
6. The Environment   68
7. Diversity in Life   80
8. Humanitarianism   99
9. Happiness and Wellbeing   112
10. Humanity and 2023/24   122

Bibliography   137
About the Author   143

ACKNOWLEDGMENTS
- APPRECIATION AND THANKS FOR SHARING THE JOURNEY WITH ME

This short book is dedicated to all those people who are awakening to the notion of Australia becoming a Republic, much sooner than later. It's dedicated to all those people who see the big picture; embrace our Indigenous history; yearn for change; are proud of their difference, and/or operate from a space of global responsibility. It takes courage to tell a story about the future but if no one else is telling the story, then how can we become the greater beholders of our stories and influence change. It is much easier for people to criticise and tear you down rather than prop you up and praise you for your insights, talents and skills.

I'd like to think that we are a nation with a heartfelt vision for the future. Thank you to the following people who have not criticised me but rather through their inspiration and encouragement have helped me to self publish the material in this book:

- My my mum Astrid for her valued love and support.
- Cem for your idea and inspiration to take what has already been written and put it into a revised form.
- John Bond from the Republic of Australia facebook site for your encouragement and guidance.
- Rob Williams, for book cover design Fiverr.com/cal5086.

All quotes and references are made with admiration and respect (without any particular permission) but with no intention of infringement of copyright.

And finally, special thanks to you the readers, for your openness, patience, and support. I hope this book provides something different and unique but ultimately inspires hope.

Dedicated with much love and blessings. David

Visit me at: www.davidshaunlarsen.com
 Email: davidsdm@yahoo.com

INTRODUCTION

- THE RISE OF THE GREAT SOUTHERN LAND

I have a vision for Australia and it's a new story, about a new chapter for our great nation but its more than a dream, it foretells our destiny. *'The Rise of the Great Southern Land"* is my second book and interweaves a mix of stories into a series of chapters to provide a 5-year blueprint for how Australia will become a Republic by January 26th, 2023. However, this short book is more than a blueprint, it describes our Dreamtime, our connection to something much much greater. Our nation is crying out for change, simply put leadership. I can assure you the forces of change are coming but we must Awaken to our collective responsibilities as people and communities, who can unite in action as One. Come join me.

I am a futurist let's say forward-thinking and strategic but can see things that others don't. We all have the same ability and skill. It's just about observing or scratching beneath the surface to observe what lies underneath the things that we see and witness. The rest is easy, connect the dots, be brave, show courage and then tell a story. My triple great Grandfather Sir Henry Parkes was a visionary man and I am embarrassed that few Australians know of him or realise that he is the Father of our Federation. What does that say about us as a nation in understanding our history? Parkes had a vision that our former colonies would unite as one great nation. Parkes stated that "surely what the Americans did by war, Australians can bring about in peace".

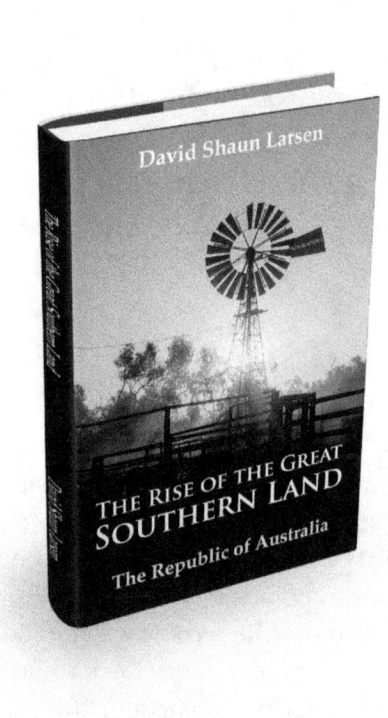

Parkes was a great statesman, orator and among many things fought for educational reform, jobs and fair wages, created Centennial Park and helped form the ideals of our modern democracy. However, he wasn't perfect and at that time, he believed this new nation should be racially homogeneous. It's now time that we grow up and mature as a nation and also tell the story of the intergenerational trauma that our Indigenous people experienced and own it.

No one can tell me that he or she can't read the "Uluru Statement from the Heart" and not feel ashamed, guilt or feel sorry. I feel deep empathy and the wounds run deep, for the death and suffering our First Nation peoples have endured. I'm tired and disgusted as an Australian when I hear people say "Why can't they just move on". I have met few people who even know of the Uluru Statement never alone who have read it. Ignorance is bliss but it is dangerous, I'd like to think we are not a nation of stupid people.

The only way we can heal our past is to become a Republic and have our Indigenous people at the heart our new constitution. It is the most logical, fair and heartfelt solution. It won't affect anyone's dignity or lives for that matter. If anything we can have pride in knowing that we are the most modern leading democracy on our planet and unite as one just in the same way our politicians united in passing Marriage Equality. It was joyful, a moment of bipartisan politics, to see our politicians united and what a beautiful message this sends to our children. The message is that there is hope in this world, as long as you fight for something with the right intention, from a space of love as opposed to fear. If we can do the same for our new constitution, imagine the power of that and what we may witness.

> Run your fingers through my soul.
> For once, just once,
> feel exactly what I feel,
> believe what I believe,
> perceive as I perceive,
> look, experience, examine,
> and for once;
> just once,
> Understand...

Australia needs to celebrate our multiculturalism for we are the most multicultural nation on earth and we always have been. Even before settlement there were 250 great nations crossing this vast land

and that in itself is impressive but sounds pretty challenging. Imagine if Europe had 250 countries, it may have been the battleground for more than two world wars. Did you know there are more than 200 languages spoken every day in Australia - about 70 of these are Aboriginal, and approximately 130 are European and Asian.

Let's move forward and celebrate with joy and be proud that we have the oldest continuous spiritual culture on earth. It is time that we unite and all walk across this vast country together and pay our respects to our elders both past and present, no matter where we come from. We are all interconnected and once you understand the oneness that we have with this Great Southern land, our spiritual journey will continue just as it always has and always will.

1

AUSTRALIAN INDIGENOUS CULTURE
- THE OLDEST CONTINUOUS SPIRITUAL CULTURE ON EARTH

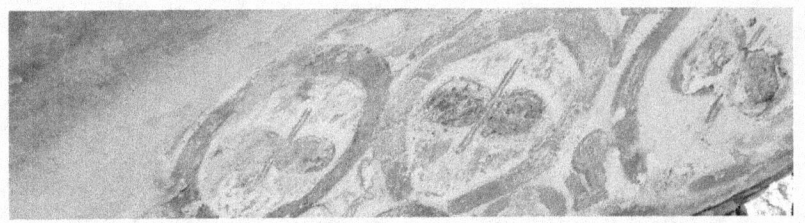

> *Proportionally, we are the most incarcerated people on the planet... Our children are alienated from their families at unprecedented rates... And our youth languish in detention in obscene numbers. They should be our hope for the future. These dimensions of our crisis tell plainly the structural nature of our problem... In 1967 we were counted, in 2017 we seek to be heard. We leave base camp and start our trek across this vast country. We invite you to walk with us in a movement of the Australian people for a better future.*
>
> — The Uluru Statement from The Heart

I respectively advise Aboriginal and Torres Strait Islander people that this chapter may contain images of deceased indigenous people and ask that you read this with caution.

The Failing of our Education System

The failing of our education system is exemplified by how little young people know about history. I attended school in Mount Isa, and I learned surprisingly little; if anything that I can remember about our Aboriginal and Torres Strait Islander (ABSTI) people, culture or history. Mount Isa and the surrounding region was home to the **Kalkadoon** (properly **Kalkatungu**) who ruled what is called the emu foot province and were living on these lands for over 40 thousand years. Their forefather tribe have been called 'the elite of the Aboriginal warriors of Queensland'.[1]

> The Kalkadoon's acknowledged a leader, and they always knew precisely where he was located. Once or twice a year delegates from the wandering bands of Kalkadoon people would assemble at the leader's camp and be instructed on raids or attacks on neighbours and at times two or more of these wandering bands would join forces.
>
> — Chern'ee Sutton Contemporary Aboriginal Artist

They would rarely leave their country, they protected their land ferociously and were known to surrounding tribes as fearsome warriors.[2]

The Kalkadoon people were fiercely independent and would mark the boundaries of their territory with an emu or cranes foot that was either painted on to rocks or trees or carved on to the sold granite rock as a warning to other intruding clans. Interestingly, they would rotate their campsites for a few weeks at a time and live off the land until their resources became scarce and not return for 2 or 3 years, so the wildlife and vegetation could replenish and survive.[2]

This story inherently speaks to our Indigenous people's respect for the land and ability to live alongside nature, honouring the delicate equilibrium that existed with our ecosystem. Such incredible people! The older I get, I always have my eyes very wide open. I am eager to learn and have an intense thirst for understanding and knowing more about our Indigenous people, their culture, traditions and maybe even one day their languages. I have learned more since leaving school, yet I am still amazed at how little I don't know.

I'm in awe of the 250 or more nations that once crossed our continent (and still do to varying degrees today); the diversity of its people and languages; their storytelling; enormous respect for their Elders and aboriginal art, music, spirituality and even weaponry, mining, farming, and sport. On the darker side, I have also learned about our ingrained racism as a nation. This dark side includes their untold genocide; dispossession and incarceration as people; the endless lists of deaths in custody; extinction of the Tasmanian aboriginals; the stolen generation; their fight to be counted as people and our nation's struggle to Close the Gap on our ABSTI people's health and life expectancy.

Image of a Warrior of the Kalkadoon People - Kerry Photo Sydney. Charles Henry 1857-1928

As I write this book and start talking about this chapter with people I meet; I'm still so surprised and amazed at people's ignorance. To be honest, I'm so sick and tired of Australia's ignorance and people who continue to perpetuate this myth of a "hand out mentality" that our Indigenous people supposedly have. Often their defence is not grounded in any reality and is always based on some experience from their childhood or hearing about abuse, violence or what has happened to a third party person, friend or relative. There is also this perception of favouritism, that they deserve something more than me and questioning, "Why do I always have to identify on official forms whether I am either ABSTI or not?".

A photograph of my dear nephew Linkyn (aged 11) playing the digeridoo. He is very proud of his Indigenous culture and history.

It's so demoralising and mortifying to me; it's no wonder I am writing this chapter in the hope that it's not too late to progress the healing and reconciliation process. In all these situations, I just wish I could say, "I'm Indigenous" like my 11- year-old nephew Linkyn does, who proudly wears his Indigenous status on his sleeve. It melts away any form of racism when he smiles and says these words; it makes people think and challenges the stereotypical views. Most people still can't seem to apprehend that ABSTI Australians can be of any colour whether black, brown, white or any shade of grey.

I hope one day, someone like our great film director Bruce Beresford (who recently remade the famous "Roots" miniseries of the 1970s) or an up and coming Indigenous film director, can tell our own story not too dissimilar to "Roots" i.e., tell the story of our the intergenerational trauma our Indigenous people experienced from settlement right up until the Referendum of 1967 or even better to when we become a Republic. It's all about the symbolism, nothing more, nothing less; once people realise it, we can all move on together!

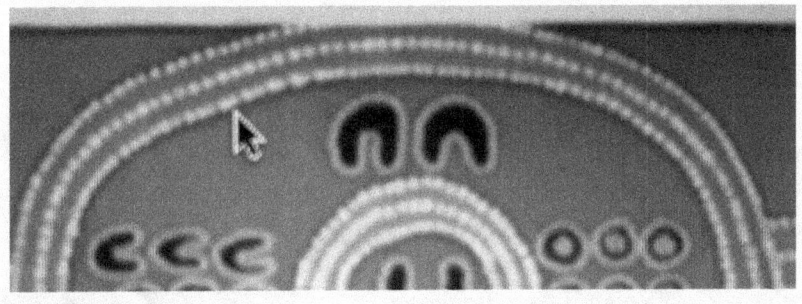

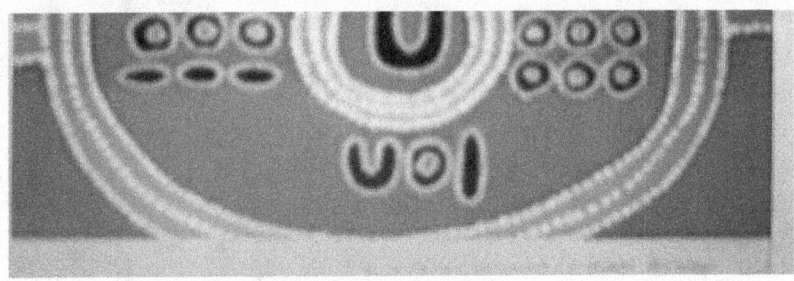

Two halves of an Indigenous Art painting deliberately shown as broken; to represent how far we have not come regarding Constitutional Reform in Australia.

The Uluru Statement

Hundreds of Aboriginal community leaders met at Uluru in late May 2017 to find common ground on a way forward. This capped off a dozen regional meetings around the country.

Our Aboriginal and Torres Strait Islander tribes were the first sovereign Nations of the great Australian continent and its adjacent islands, and possessed it under our own laws and customs. This our ancestors did, according to the reckoning of our culture, from the

Creation, according to the common law from 'time immemorial', and according to science more than 60,000 years ago.

This sovereignty is *a spiritual notion: the ancestral tie between the land, or 'mother nature', and the Aboriginal and Torres Strait Islander peoples who were born therefrom, remain attached thereto, and must one day return thither to be united with our ancestors. This link is the basis of the ownership of the soil, or better, of sovereignty.* It has never been ceded or extinguished, and co-exists with the sovereignty of the Crown.

How could it be otherwise? That peoples possessed a land for sixty millennia and this sacred link disappears from world history in merely the last two hundred years?

With substantive constitutional change and structural reform, we believe this ancient sovereignty can shine through as a fuller expression of Australia's nationhood.

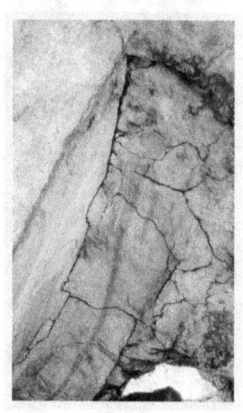

Indigenous rock art The Kimberley, Western Australia

Proportionally, we are the most incarcerated people on the planet. We are not an innately criminal people. Our children are alienated from their families at unprecedented rates. This cannot be because we have no love for them. And our youth languish in detention in obscene numbers. They should be our hope for the future.

These dimensions of our crisis tell plainly the structural nature of our problem. This is *the torment of our powerlessness.*

We seek constitutional reforms to empower our people and take *a rightful place* in our own country. When we have power over our destiny our children will flourish. They will walk in two worlds and their culture will be a gift to their country.

We call for the establishment of a **First Nations Voice enshrined in the Constitution.**

Makarrata is the culmination of our agenda: *the coming together after a struggle.* It captures our aspirations for a fair and truthful relationship with the people of Australia and a better future for our children based on justice and self-determination.

We seek a Makarrata Commission to supervise a process of agreement-making between governments and First Nations and truth-telling about our history.

In 1967 we were counted, in 2017 we seek to be heard. **We leave base camp and start our trek across this vast country. We invite you to walk with us in a movement of the Australian people for a better future.**

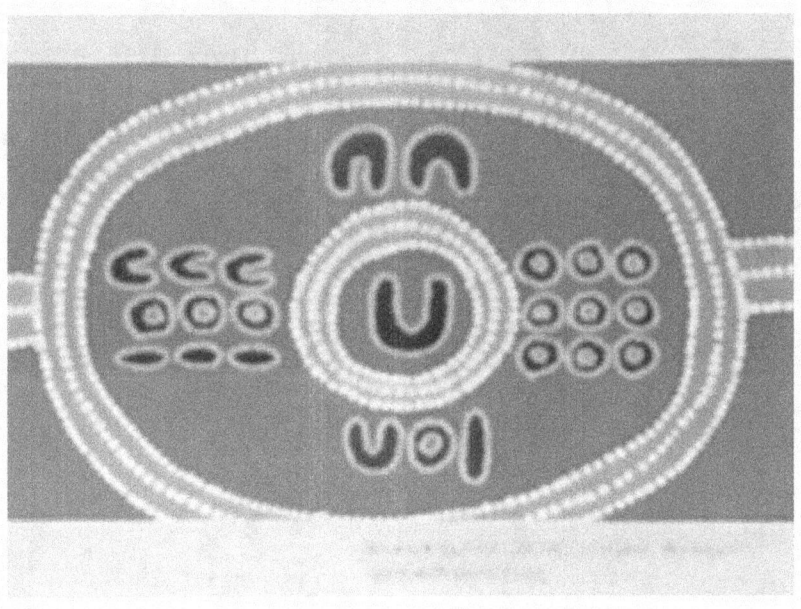

The same Indigenous Art painting brought together to represent the Unity of Constitutional Reform in Australia.

Welome to Our Past

Welcome to our past, let's suspend disbelief but imagine that you (including the cultural heritage that you may identify with) belong to the oldest, continuous spiritual culture on earth. Imagine that one day, your land was invaded and you were brutally forced to change the way you live, and behave and become disconnected from the spiritual essence and heart of who you were as a person. Welcome to the past…

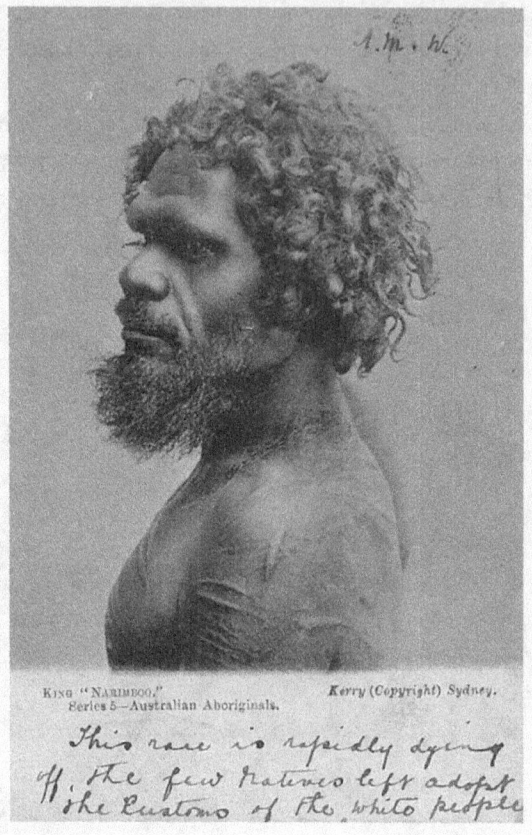

King "Narimboo" Aboriginal Man, Fine Art America.

"This race is rapidly dying off; the few natives left to adopt the customs of the white people" - an example of the sheer racism that existed.

As a result of this you were literally forced into a state of despair and victimisation, which included: -

- **Death from new diseases;**
- **Forcibly displaced off your traditional land** (your home and that of generations before you);
- **Suffered genocide** (some estimates of over 500,000 people or even more, we may never know); **65,180 is the number of Aboriginal Australians, historians estimate were killed in**

Queensland alone from the 1820s until the early 1900s [3]. You work out the maths...
- **Treated as a basic barbarian** (the lowest of low life);
- **Deliberately not allowed by law to education** and
- **Not even worthy of being counted as a person**, in what we so-called, a civilised nation.

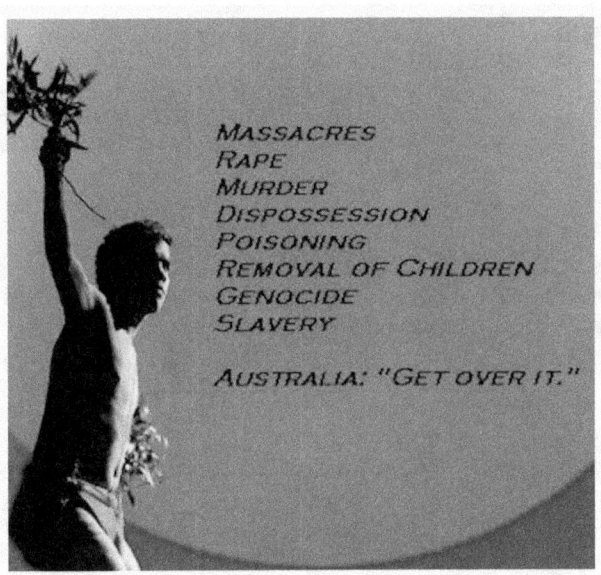

Lastly, to top it off, in today's Australia, you then embody the most extreme statistics of drug and alcohol misuse, male suicide, domestic violence, HIV infection and living with chronic diseases. But sorry to finally put a nail in the coffin; you also become the most incarcerated people on our earth and die much earlier than most people around you.

Intergenerational trauma is something inescapable that all Australians need to finally understand and the effects that it has had on our Indigenous people. We must also stop questioning why Indigenous Australians can't just "get over it" and "move on". The impact of colonisation (our invasion) and the horrifying abuse and dreadful atrocities that were committed in the past, continue to this day to contribute to some of the most significant health and social inequalities than in any other western nation. For example, poor health outcomes compared to non-Aboriginal Australians, including an average life expectancy for males that is 21 years less and for females almost 20 years less than the total population.[4]

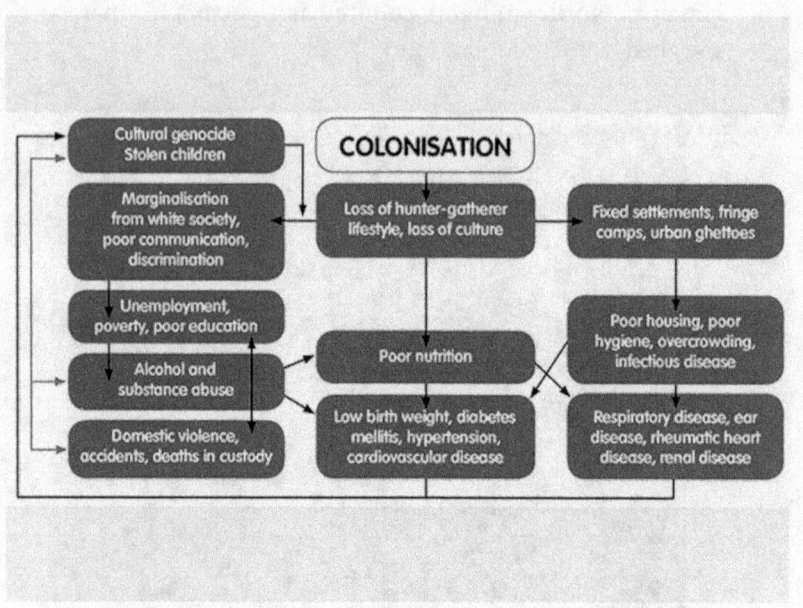

The effects of Intergenerational trauma - a visual guide that explains why we need to man up as a nation.

> The trauma and suffering that Indigenous people have experienced over generations have contributed to the burden of disease, substance misuse, and incarceration
>
> — AUSTRALIANSTOGETHER.ORG.AU

Pause for a moment, because this is disturbing and even writing about it creates such a pain in my heart; for I am not proud to be an Australian, not in a country that controls our civil liberties and dictates our rights. What is even more troubling is how we allow our politicians that we elect to create, legislate and tell our story. That's the greatest irony, and we are only perpetuating it.

If this doesn't create a shiver, trauma, and pain, at the deepest level and heart of your psyche, how can we honestly truly be responsible as Australians for our destiny? We need to finally name it for what it is, speak with truth and compassion and search deep in our souls. This is not about an apology, empowerment, rights or reconciliation but it's about something that is far greater and much more powerful. It's speaking to the soul of our nation which is crying for hope and restoration. This is our moment for transformation so that we can become attuned to the spirituality of our great land. It's the land of our Indigenous people, it always has and always will.

Through the Uluru statement, our Indigenous people sought to become heard. They have the compassion to embrace us, for they see the future and know we can become one and walk together on our journey. Hence why it is a **Statement from The Heart**. They know the soul and spirit of our great nation is broken, and we need to finally man and woman up; because if you genuinely want to make a difference in this world, it starts right here, right now and in this nation.

We can no longer gloss over the past, for this past is one of the greatest travesties in our human history. The only decent, mature and right thing we can do is pay our respects to all our Elders past and present and raise our Indigenous people out of this dark history of abuse, hate, bigotry, and discrimination and allow them the dignity to reclaim their heart. As Sir Henry Parkes (our Father of Federation) said about the great nation he imagined, and we created in a former time, for a former people,

> Surely what the Americans did by war, Australians can bring about in peace

— Sir Henry Parkes, Father of Federation,
Tenterfield Oration, 1889

The Australian constitution was created for a nation that was built for a former time. My triple great, grandfather Sir Henry Parkes had a vision for Australia as a union of a disparate group of colonies, without respect for our Indigenous culture. What we need to do today is to tell the new story of what our great nation could become. What would that story be? Well, the story I want to tell is of the Republic of

Australia, which embraces our Indigenous people at the heart of our new constitution. It is a story that tells the truth about settlement and the powerlessness of the struggle of our Indigenous people; yet tells a story of our spirituality, the love for our children and hope for the future.

Indigenous Rock Art The Kimberley, Western Australia (W.A.) - is a sparsely settled northern region of W.A. It's known for large areas of wilderness; defined by rugged mountains, dramatic gorges, semi-savanna and isolated coastline.

Therefore, surely what we can now do as a nation is bring about constitutional change, nothing more, nothing less. We can only do this if we start telling a new story, and not just imagine it but make it happen. We need to stop contributing to the myths that we cannot create change, for if you speak up and demand change, you can create the new story for our nation and that of our Indigenous people.

There is no greater agony than bearing the untold story of what our great nation could've become. It's time that the former great Indigenous nations of Australia are recognised and embodied at the heart of our new constitution. We need to walk with our Indigenous people in a new movement. This movement is the emergence of a new 21st century nation, the great Republic of Australia.

Let's Start Dispelling the Myths

Let's start dispelling the myths as there are many things about Indigenous history that you probably didn't learn about in school. Indigenous rights campaigner Julian Cleary outlines some of these below. Cleary says they are some of the most interesting, humbling, and inspiring facts that have been whitewashed from our history lessons.[5]

Martumili Ngurra canvass National Museum of Australia - A bearded Aboriginal man, walking among long grass with a smoking stick.

- **You learnt about the First Fleet. You didn't learn about Indigenous settlements.** Early explorers described Indigenous, irrigation systems, agriculture and grain harvest right across Australia. 30,000-year-old grindstones have been found near Walgett, NSW, and ancient stone fish traps at Brewarrina, NSW; may be the oldest human-made structures on earth. And today at Budj Bim, Victoria, you can visit the remains of stone houses and an aquaculture system that pre-date Egypt's pyramids by at least 4,000 years.
- **You learnt about Matthew Flinders. You didn't learn about Aboriginal international trade connections.** Well before

British invasion, Yolngu and other Aboriginal groups exchanged goods, ideas and culture with Macassan sailors from what is now Sulawesi, Indonesia. The Macassans arrived in search of sea cucumber (trepang) to trade in China. In 1803 when Matthew Flinders was circumnavigating the country, he met a Macassan fisherman who told Flinders he had been harvesting trepang on the northern shores of Australia for 20 years. This story lives on in the ceremony and language of the Yolngu.

- **You learnt how to play Aussie Rules Football. You didn't learn about Marngrook.** Marngrook is a game played by Aboriginal groups across southern Australia. This almost certainly influenced Australian rules football, although the Australian Football League still disputes this. The 'Protector of Aborigines' and author William Thomas wrote about an Aboriginal football match played at Pound Bend, Victoria, in 1852. Thomas wrote that the players kicked the possum-skin ball high with the instep of the foot and "leap as high as five feet or more from the ground to catch the ball". Tom Wills, credited as one of the founders of Aussie rules, lived in the Grampians (Gariwerd) as a young man. He reportedly grew up surrounded by Djab wurrung children, learnt their language fluently and played Marngrook with them.

- **You learnt about cowboys and Indians. You didn't learn about Aboriginal resistance leaders.** In the late 19th century, Jandamarra and the Bunuba People resisted the violent encroachment of squatters onto their country in the Kimberley. Jandamarra had been a talented police tracker, but his people were being shot and poisoned, and the survivors were being enslaved around him. "Jandamarra died on his own soil defending his country. A true Australian hero." Paul Kelly, Singer/Songwriter.

- **You learnt about the suffragette and civil rights movement. You didn't learn about the Aboriginal and Torres Strait Islander civil rights movement.** It wasn't until the federal election in 1963 that all Aboriginal and Torres Strait Islander adults were able to vote – more than 50 years after Australian women got that right. This was the year Martin Luther King gave his "I have a dream" speech. At the same time in Australia, there was a growing movement of Indigenous activists and supporters demanding civil rights.

Dreamtime Sisters by Colleen Wallace Nungari.

There are so many other historical moments in our Aboriginal and Torres Strait Islander people's history and struggle for human rights. These moments cannot be adequately covered in this chapter. It's our inherent responsibility as Australians to learn, know and understand about our Indigenous Australian history. The sheer importance of this is something that we cannot ignore for it will enrich us all as people, and I throw down the gauntlet for you to find out more.

Constitutional change is possible

Constitutional change is possible and is something that is imperative for our Nation, following The Referendum 1957-1967. In 1967, after ten years of campaigning, a referendum was held to change the Australian Constitution. Two negative references to Aboriginal Australians were removed, giving the Commonwealth the power to legislate for them as a group. This change was seen by many as a recognition of Aboriginal people as full Australian citizens. The referendum campaign effectively focused public attention on the fact that Aboriginal and Torres Strait Islander Australians were second-class citizens with all sorts of limitations - legislative and social - on their lives.[6]

 The Dreaming means our identity as people, the cultural teaching and everything that's part of our lives here, you know?...it's the understanding of what we have around us

— MERV PENRITH (WALLAGA LAKE, 1996)

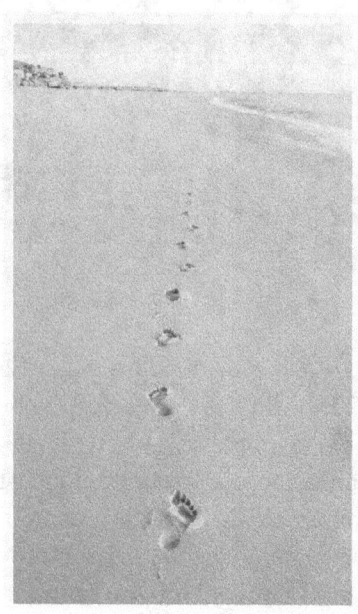

It's time that our Indigenous people are recognised, and we walk with them in a new movement for change.

Australians are well known for our relaxed and easy-going nature. Where do you think we get this from as a nation? We have lived side by side our Indigenous People for 200 years or more, and I'd like to think that THEIR easy going natures have rubbed off on us somewhat. Our Indigenous people have always had a chilled and relaxed way of being and in many ways the expression, "She'll be right mate" is symbolic of this. Fellow Aussies will know that it can either refer to an outlook of optimism or apathy i.e., whatever is wrong will right itself with time. Professor Sussex [7] said in the Sydney Morning Herald before colonisation there were about 250 Aboriginal languages in Australia.

There are more than 200 languages spoken every day in Australia - about 70 of these are Aboriginal, and approximately 130 are European and Asian.

We are also known for our love of dolphins, dugongs and whales; it's like it's ingrained in our DNA and we will fiercely do anything to protect them. I'd like to think that we get this from our Indigenous cultures, as they have lived side by side with our whales, dolphins, and dugongs for thousands of years. Think of Hervey Bay in Queensland which is the gateway to K'gari (Fraser Island) - the national park that spans pretty much most of Fraser Island has been renamed "K'gari". This has been a partial victory for the Butchulla people (traditional owners) who are campaigning to rename the whole island. Hervey Bay is also home to the annual whale migration from Antartica. Anywhere where mother whales go (and feel safe enough for 4 months of the year) to have their baby calves, nurture them, then begin the migration south; must be a special, spiritual "energetic centre".

Lake Mackenzie, K'Gari (Fraser Island). K'Gari is home to the Butchulla people.

The Butchulla people have always known this and have revered the whales. Many streets and landmarks in Hervey Bay also have Aboriginal names. Hervey Bay even has a "Paddle Out for Whales" which is an annual event held in the whale watching capital of the world, as part of IFAW's National Whale Day celebrations. The event is held to help raise awareness of the many issues whales face today. The number and diversity of events all over the country on the day illustrates how valuable whales are to Australians in our unity and commitment to protecting them.[8]

A lot has been covered in this chapter, and I hope the readers are left with some valuable insights into the rich culture, history, and resilience of our Indigenous people. Our Aboriginal and Torres Strait Islander people are the fastest growing population group in Australia, and I think it's time that the Great Nations of our Indigenous people are recognised and embodied at the heart of our New Constitution. Let's walk with our Indigenous people in a New Movement for change. Let's make what seems to be Impossible, Possible.

Our Dreamtime - let's leave base camp together and start our trek across this vast country. We are all interconnected and once you understand the oneness we have with this great land our spiritual journey will continue like it always has.

2

POLITICS FOR OUR AGE
- A NEW POLITICAL MOVEMENT FOR THE 21ST CENTURY

> *The great question…is whether the time has not now arisen for the creation of this Australian continent of an Australian Government and an Australian Parliament. I believe the time has come.*
>
> — Sir Henry Parkes, Tenterfield Oration, 1889

Has Politics Lost its Way?

Has politics lost its way? Politics as a movement and system has lost its way, and real meaning for the average Australian or American for that matter and this profoundly resonates in the hearts of most of us. Both countries are portrayed prominently in this chapter, as our people are crying out for change but be careful about what you ask or how you vote.

Sir Henry Parkes

We only have three options. We can either become beacons of left-wing political change, that protects our civil liberties and focusses on true prosperity for all or right-wing ideology and extremism that always operates from a space of judgement, hate and fear - a divide and conquer mentality. Our democracy, civil liberties, and freedoms are far more critical. The middle path or centre of politics is the third option (very Buddhist in principle). However, when the pendulum has swung too far one way, it tends to seek balance and swings back the other way to establish the radical change we need; before finding the harmonious balance between the two extremes.

For a nation that parodies disinterest in politics; Australia uncannily divests an enormous amount of our energy, conversation and time complaining about it! In many ways, the apathy and disregard for politics among the electorate is very disturbing and not surprisingly feeds directly into the hands of the power moguls i.e., the corrupt corporations, lobbyists, and an array of disenchanted groups that rally to the cause. Also, the economic pessimism that permeates our societies today and the fear of impending change - not dissimilar to a readjustment that we might need to make - if we experience a sudden life event, illness or even ageing itself. Adjusting to change is something that can occur over a short period or with rapid onset.

The readjustment that our society needs to undertake as we make a transition from one economic period to another will be a painful and challenging experience for most people. I fear that we are about to enter a period of significant economic readjustment. The election of Malcolm Turnbull as Prime Minister in Australia and Donald Trump as President of the United States has been anything but disappointing for both countries. However disappointing it may be; the significance of these men coming into power is also a positive for the world, as it feeds the movement for critical change that is desperately needed.

Malcolm Turnbull was posing for a selfie on Twitter for APEC 2017 - later it was revealed that there was one more person who had posed for the selfie, only to be cropped out (Vietnamese President Tran Dai Quang). Vietnam was the host of APEC.

   Malcolm Turnbull   @TurnbullMalcolm - Catching up with @realDonaldTrump & President Xi at #APEC2017; working together to secure our region's safety & prosperity

These type of men only operate with selfish intent, putting self-interest above everything else. So what is selfish intent and what does it look like? Recently there was an infamous selfie taken by Malcolm

Turnbull at APEC in November 2017. There is nothing wrong with an odd selfie now and again. However this selfie was deplorable, later it was revealed that the Vietnamese president Tran Dai Quang had also posed for the selfie (he got cropped out). Some may argue that this is insignificant, but it's not when Vietnam was also the host nation for APEC.

Somehow I don't think this is working together to secure our region's safety & prosperity, especially when the host nation is viewed as lesser significant.

Let's Go Onward Together

Let's go Onward Together. The election of Donald Trump is not the beginning of a new era; it's the beginning of the end. It's more the end of an old era, with the death throes of right-wing conservatism in the world e.g., it becomes the vehicle that will finally take down right-wing conservative politics in the next generation.

Onward Together slogan

Whenever we try to release any old pattern of thinking or ways of working; the situation seems to get tenser for awhile, until we settle into the new situation. Our response in times of change is to react naturally! When we embrace change with positivity and move forward, we're developing something counter to the old ways of thinking.

Therefore, what the world needs is a new Counter-Revolution, to change this sad state of affairs. Hillary Clinton officially announced in May 2017 the formation of a new political organisation aimed at funding "resistance groups" standing up to President Donald Trump.

The idea for a Clinton political group started after Hilary Clinton met with a group of young activists. She, therefore, launched "Onward Together" as a way to encourage people to get involved, to organise, and even run for office.[9] "Onward Together" was in essence, a way for the Democrats to boost their electoral hopes while subtly questioning Trump's authenticity. Clinton certainly doesn't want to be silent in the coming years, and she wrote,

> Onward Together is dedicated to advancing the vision that earned nearly 66 million votes in the last election. By encouraging people to organize, get involved, and run for office, Onward Together will advance progressive values and work to build a brighter future for generations to come...
>
> From the Women's March to airports where communities are welcoming immigrants and refugees to town hall meetings in every community, Americans are speaking up and speaking out like never before.
>
> The challenges we face as a country are real. But there's no telling what we can achieve if we approach the fights ahead with the passion and determination we feel today, and bring that energy into 2017, 2018, 2020, and beyond.
>
> — HILLARY RODHAM CLINTON, ONWARD TOGETHER

Where are Our Leaders?

Where are our leaders? Politicians have lost the ability to lead. There seems to be a need to motivate and spur up activism among young people. In Australia with compulsory voting, there are believed to be close to 800,000 young people under 30 who have not registered to vote and if they did; they could change the outcome of the next election. Cuts this year to the Australian Electoral Commission, framed as a restructure to the Northern Territory based office also means that the Commission doesn't have the staffing to track people who haven't registered to vote. Therefore, what a perfect way to influence the outcome of the next election. I guess if you assume most people under 30 are slightly more left-leaning than it makes sense for a right-leaning party in power to try and do everything possible to stay in power.

Bernie Sanders who at 75 was the longest-serving independent in U.S. congressional history and ran for office as the Democratic Nominee up against Hilary Clinton

All around the world, people are rising to define a new vision for our collective future. What Australia needs is its own Bernie Saunders whether a man or woman, who at 75 was the longest-serving independent in U.S. congressional history running for President of the United States.

Why does there seem to be such a lacklustre pool of Australian political leaders? Have they been mostly constrained by towing the party line or possibly unable to lead, because of the ineffective political system itself? Also, the influences of news and media; the reliability and factualness of information and where people source their information from, is potentially dumbing us down. Lack of knowledge ends up satisfying our craving thirst as a people that are viewed by many politicians as "stupid". For all intended purposes, we then only have ourselves to blame, as we get the culture and political system that we deserve. The charity sector in Australia, one of the last cornerstones of our civil society and democracy, is now under attack. The Liberal Government in Australia is targeting community organisations who engage in advocacy on public policy issues. How low can a government go, it's fundamentally repulsive?

Yes there are a lot of "stupid" people in Australia and the US for that matter, and forgive me, but I mean "stupid" in the nicest possible way. I have been one of those stupid people in the past, not concerned about the bigger picture, our democracy or trying to make sense out of the fake pledges made by our politicians. Therefore by "stupid"; I'm referring to the decent, common-sense people (that part of society), that care more for the distractions of life that feed our ego rather than our minds and spirit. Politicians will always tell you what you want to hear but look behind the meaning; does it come from a space of compassion and unity or does it come from a space of judgement, division, and hate. You are a greater fool if you rally to the cause of the latter.

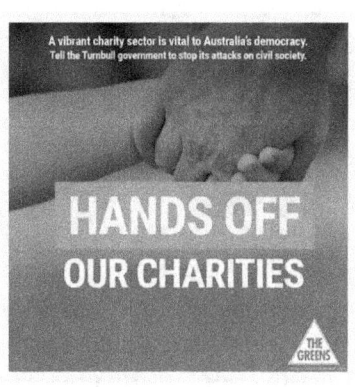

The Charity Sector is one of the cornerstones of our democracy. The Liberal Government is now targeting community organisations who engage in advocacy on public policy issues.

"Intention" in life is everything; the "right intention" is the part and sum of us that cares very deeply about our culture, our way of life and inherent values. I fear countries like the US are closer to a situation of a civil war. Trump's vision for America can't exist alongside the progressive vision created by Obama. One or the other has to prevail in the next few years. And this is what precisely happened in the lead up to the US Civil War 1861-1865. After a long-standing controversy over slavery, state's rights, protectionism and American nationalism, war broke out in April 1861. Let's hope the past does not repeat itself.

Sir Henry Parkes my Great, Great, Great Grandfather

Sir Henry Parkes my Great, Great, Great Grandfather, was an incredible man with a vision. Politics runs deep in my blood. Sir Henry Parkes was an inspiring leader and the father of our Federation (my

Uncle who lives in the US used to refer to him, as the George Washington of Australia). Sir Henry Parkes was the longest serving Premier of any state or former colony in Australia and was Premier of New South Wales on five separate occasions. Parkes also had many other talents, one of which was as a writer, which is extraordinary for someone who lacked any formal education. Maybe politics and writing is my calling too!

Sir Henry Parkes contribution to Australian politics and way of life was extraordinary. Parkes was dedicated to the idea of keeping Australian society racially homogeneous and sincere in his chosen role as guardian of the constitutional convention.[10] At the time of Federation there were estimated to be only 60,000 Indigenous people left. This is vastly reduced from the number of 250,000-750,000 at settlement (or even higher in other estimates)[11]. Let's not gloss over these facts.

The Centennial Park Trust in Sydney has listed seven reasons why Parkes was such a prominent figure in Australian politics.[12]

Statue of Sir Henry Parkes, Centennial Park, Sydney

Here are the seven reasons:

- **Rags to Riches Tale–** born into poverty, Parkes had very

little formal education, suffered early setbacks with business failure in England and came to Australia as a penniless immigrant in 1839.
- **Determined and Hard Working** – despite an early life of hardship and supporting a young family, Parkes worked odd jobs as a labourer, factory worker, shopkeeper, and journalist.
- **Held Ideas and Ideals** – he started a newspaper *The Empire* in the 1850s which were destined to be the chief organ of mid-century liberalism. He also helped set up the Australian League to educate people about the rights and duties of citizens in a democracy. He fought for jobs and fair wages by opposing the free labour, sourced through convict transportation. He argued for universal suffrage.
- **Stood for Public Office often without Personal Gain** – he sought out and was elected to the NSW Parliament in 1854 and represented his constituents for long periods without pay. He left public office on some occasions to stave off personal bankruptcy and financial problems.
- **Worked His Way to the Top** – he chaired a committee to investigate the condition of the working classes (especially his concern for children). He brought the first nursing sisters who trained under Florence Nightingale out to Australia. Parkes also was instrumental in educational reform, as he believed teachers should be remunerated for their work.
- **Great Speech Making Ability** – despite a lack of education, Parkes developed great oratory skills to inspire, unite and impel his audiences to action. Many of his speeches linger long in Australian history, and his *Tenterfield Oration* in 1889 was possibly the most influential speech that eventually led to the uniting of the colonies and the Federation of the nation of Australia.
- **Creation of Centennial Park** – the famous Centennial Park in Sydney (along with other public spaces) was one of his crowning achievements. The Park was established to commemorate the 100th anniversary of European settlement in the colony. At its opening in 1888, Parkes stated,

This grand park is emphatically the People's Park, and you must always take as much interest in it as if by your own hands you had planted the flowers, the park will be one of the grandest adornments to this beautiful country.

— Sir Henry Parkes

Statue of Sir Henry Parkes, Centennial Park Trust, Sydney

There is nothing to fear about the future if you just scratch the surface and look for the connections, you will see that there is a rich story to be told that beholds the fabric of our great nation. I believe the personal transformation the planet needs is taking place in Australia, Asia, Europe and the US. There are hints, all around us, of what will occur or is needed to happen in the world. The Brexit vote in England; the election of Donald Trump; The North Korean nuclear threat; the rise of Russia and the more significant economic alliance between China and Europe are just the beginning of the end of this era. These events are going to bring some of the most expected and unexpected convulsions, that world has ever seen. These events will also produce some of the most significant changes in the world and although we shouldn't be fearful of the consequences, those who have "Awakened" will welcome them with great opportunity. There is nothing to fear about the future. Once we emerge out of this time, we will observe some of the most accelerated changes we will ever witness on our planet in our lifetime.

 We are suffering just now from a bad attack of economic

pessimism. It is common to hear people say that the epoch of enormous economic progress which characterized the 19th century is over; that the rapid improvement in the standard of life is now going to slow down—at any rate in Great Britain; that a decline in prosperity is more likely than an improvement in the decade which lies ahead of us.

I believe that this is a wildly mistaken interpretation of what is happening to us. We are suffering, not from the rheumatics of old age, but from the growing-pains of over-rapid changes, from the painfulness of readjustment between one economic period and another…

— JOHN MAYNARD KEYNES, ECONOMIC POSSIBILITIES FOR OUR GRANDCHILDREN (1930)

This decade is very reminiscent of the 1930's, during this era we saw the emergence of right-wing politics that gripped much of the world with fascism (the rise of Hitler, Stalin, Mussolini and Hirohito). Peter Leyden wrote in his informative article, *Why Trump's Inauguration is Not the Beginning of an Era — but the End* that, "it's easy for politicians to whip up public fears against these changes and rally people to go back to the old ways, to make America great again".[13]

The Positive Reframe: Trump does the World a great Service

The Positive Reframe: Trump does the world a great service, Leyden states that California is the future and although in many ways Trump is heading down the path of fascism it won't last long. He believes that Trump is ultimately going to do America and the world a service by becoming the vehicle for change that will finally take down right-wing conservative politics for generations. His insights are convincing for the following reasons: -

- Trump has managed to get the entire Republican conservative establishment to buy into his regime.

- By doing so, Trump is creating an administration that is all about rule; some may say dictatorship.
- Therefore Trump represents the ultimate in Corporate government control. He is blatantly selling out to the wealthy, the industries bleeding our oil and carbon and celebrating an elite style of capitalism, like an episode on a reality TV show.
- Trump will therefore completely alienate the growing political constituencies of the 21st century: the Millennial Generation, professional people, people of colour, people who value education and our wiser sex, namely women (especially those who embrace their innate power).
- Trump will eventually repulse a significant number of more moderate Republicans. And finally, the white working class people who got him elected, however they will never admit that they voted for him.
- The analogy is going to be closer to what happened to the conservative Republicans coming out of the 1930s — they were out of power for the next 50 years.

Some may counter-argue that California is not the forerunner of the future, questioning:

- Who is this process intended to be for?
- Will it feed into more inequality in the world?
- Is the issue of globalisation and capitalism driving such changes?
- Is the left being counter-intuitive to the changes it wants to create?
- Is turning to the past, not a bad thing it may not be progressive but is it regressive?

Even if these ring true, one could say; isn't it better to model some positive progress for the future that will hopefully raise humankind out of the vulnerable state of affairs our world finds itself today? All progress must start somewhere, but we need to continually ensure that it is equitable and inclusive for all, reaching all classes and the entire population of our planet.

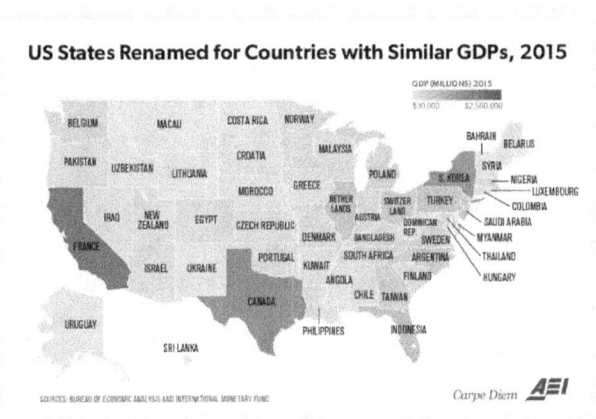

Leyden believes the backlash or counter-revolution will be fast and furious. And it won't just be Trump that goes down — it will be Prime Minister Turnbull and large swaths of conservative politicians everywhere, hopefully before it is too late for the World. I believe like Leyden that the next 3 to 6 years are going to see a severe revolutionary change in politics — to the left, not the right. It's possible that Hillary Clinton wouldn't have brought about the kind of transformation that the world currently needs. She is more likely to help the convulsion to the left by driving the "Onward Together" movement, as a grassroots activist organisation, that will rely on the further public donation if it's to be successful.

The days of conservative ideology will be long gone, the out-dated modes of working and ideas will perish and be noted only as a scholarly learning in our history books. The world needs to move on. The events leading up to Humanity and 2024 is going to bring a new leadership the world needs to enable it to make the next global shift. I believe this shift will herald an overarching energy of revolutionary change, where we will make the full transition to digital technologies; unimaginable scientific discoveries; acceptance of diversity in sexuality and culture; reshaping capitalism to rebalance massive inequalities; humanitarianism, and making a significant progression with climate change.

Let's Go Together

Let's Go Together as one and a movement for political change in the 21st century. It's necessary to go together and embrace positive change for the greater good of Humanity; progressive Governments and technological innovation. The most progressive societies on earth such as the Northern European Nations (Netherlands, Scandinavian Countries, and Germany), Canada, New Zealand, California and New York State in the US are embodying the next economic and technological period of growth. They wholeheartedly resist any political movement towards the right. Also, I believe there will be enormous political shifts occurring in Taiwan, Korea, Hong Kong, Japan, Singapore and China, although in China with increasing civil unrest. How this impacts on the world and plays out is uncertain?

Conservative ideology and politics will be a thing of the past. Australia is emerging out of this period, and places like California represent a microcosm of this, for I believe it is an "energetic centre". California has traditionally been a place that spurns a culture of innovation, new ideas, movements for change and sets trends. If you think about it, the early settlers had a sense of "Go West, young man" but those early pioneers were possibly already ahead of their time. Although framed around fertile farmlands and the need for westerly expansion, I feel California has always been something much greater, even outside of the US .

The future economy of the world is already working in California, and it has surpassed France as the world's 6th largest economy in 2016.[14] Also, for the vast majority of its citizens, Trump lost to Hillary in California by 4.3 million votes.[15]

 Resist, insist, persist, enlist

— Hillary Rodham Clinton

Now the time has come to bring about real change; all we need is a critical mass of people who care enough to create a COUNTER-REVOLUTION. Surely those people who cause so much pain in the world by preaching about division, war, and hate; WE the real people can bring about through love and understanding. The ground is fertile in this great nation for the birth of a new political force or movement for change. All we need is a new leader, statesman or stateswoman to inspire hope and lead the way.

We can't be silent anymore; we need to drive the change, we need to speak out and stand shoulder-to-shoulder and add our voices to fight for justice FOR ALL. If we are to create the Politics for Our Age, we need to start with a new political movement for the 21st century. *People just like you and me.*

 If you want to go quickly, go alone. If you want to go far, go together

— PROVERB

Play Your Part in Creating Change for Australia

3

THE REPUBLIC OF AUSTRALIA

- THE EMERGENCE OF A 21ST CENTURY NATION

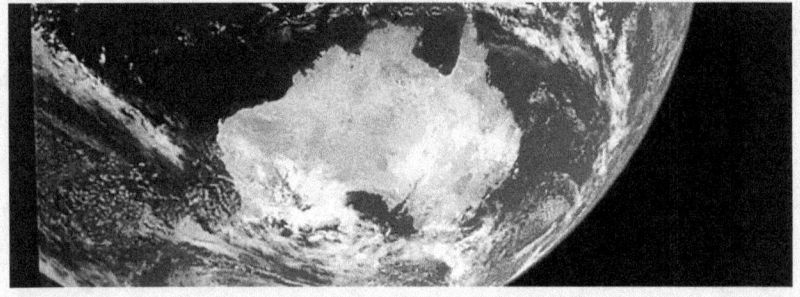

> *There is no greater agony than bearing the untold story of what our great nation could've become. If we hold it inside us; we miss out on the immense opportunity to teach future generations about our vision for Australia.*
>
> *If our next generation doesn't hear our stories, they will see us as much greater fools than what we think we are. Our future generations know that they eventually become the great beholders of our stories and destiny...*
>
> — DAVID SHAUN LARSEN

How do we describe the emergence of a 21st century Nation? There are many ways you could describe this process, but I'd rather think the emergence of a 21st century Nation describes the distinct attributes of the nation that we see Australia becoming today and over the next 5 years. This is opposed to the nation we birthed at Federation in 1901. I believe there are three distinct elements that define our modern nation, much like a trinity of energy.

A map of Australia incorporating our Aboriginal colours: Black – represents the Aboriginal people of Australia. Yellow circle – represents the Sun, the giver of life and protector. Red – represents the red earth, the red ochre used in ceremonies and Aboriginal peoples' spiritual relation to the land.
newsroom.unsw.edu.au

As a nation, we have an identity or that part of us that defines us as people and what we aspire to achieve in life and work. **This is what I call our nation's spirit.** We also have an emotional heart or that part of us that embodies our emotional feeling as a nation. This is what I call our nation's soul. Lastly, we have a persona or character, which very much describes how the world sees us as a people and a nation. This is our nation's personality vehicle or outer world identity.

If you think about it, Australia is a country that has found its modern identity through a range of attributes such as punching above its weight in terms of science and humanitarianism; experimenting with new ways of doing things; fighting to preserve its environment;

embracing computers and technology with a fervour and not to mention our sexual diversity and multiculturalism. Also like our flora and fauna, our geographic isolation has created something a little bit different when it comes to celebrating its dance music culture; rock bands, cabaret, forging its identity through cinema and interactive light displays such as 'Vivid'. We also exhibit extreme apathy towards our current nanny state and political system. All these features describe our obsession with being different and unique (what I call Aquarian in nature).

However, our nations' soul speaks to something very different, our inherent ability to reconcile the past and heal deep emotional wounds. Our nation's soul is the spiritual essence of who we are and our connection to the land; something so profound and ethereal, thus represented so symbolically by our Indigenous people and their cultures. The Oldest Continuous Spiritual Culture on Earth, that's something mighty to be proud of and celebrate with such joy and passion.

The persona or character of our nation in many ways, defines how the world sees us as a nation e.g., such as when we finally emerge as a Republic. We are seen as easy go lucky, optimistic and always coming to the aid of others when there are disasters, emergencies or war (the great rescuers). We always fight for the rights of others; love our freedom and are also characterised by many things such as our love for sport, gambling, horse racing, respect for truth and wanting fairness for all. We also don't want our politicians to give us the simple facts, for we are not that stupid. We want our politicians to tell us the detail and the truth; it's as simple as that.

The Australian Counter-Revolution - 2018-2023

Wake up Australia, the undercurrent of the Australian Counter-Revolution has started and will only escalate. In effect, it commenced in late 2017, with our postal vote for Marriage Equality (and possibly earlier last year with the Uluru Statement). The Marriage Equality postal vote has nothing to do with Marriage Equality but has everything to do with where we stand as a nation, in terms of our maturity, sense of justice and appetite for change.

Play Your Part in Creating Change for Australia

This will be followed this year or possibly next by our first recession in 27 years since June 1991. This recession will be significant for Australia, possibly quite severe and will happen under a Liberal Government. I always see recessions as great levellers, as they force us to look outwards rather than inwards. In times of recession, everyone knows someone who is doing it tough, and we can no longer rely on the old industries or ways of working e.g., mining, agriculture, and property. A recession is a catalyst for change, that births new innovative industries or ways of working.

I believe this change will be centred primarily around computers, science, technology and innovation and structural changes on a scale that we have never seen before i.e., green technology, new scientific discoveries, carbon tax, greater environmental protection, political uprising (reclaiming our civil liberties and transforming our political institutions) and many other revolutionary grass-root and innovative changes around how we live. This will also lead to massive societal changes or shifts in our national psyche; not only around the way we think but also view ourselves in the world. In many respects, it will enable us to transform ourselves as a nation, out of the "me me me" culture that we have created over the past 27 years of economic prosperity.

Therefore, what we become and how we act as a nation, will be more focussed towards the greater good of Humanity in contrast to our self-obsessed, patriarchal and inward-looking qualities as a country. But I believe more and more people will have the courage to challenge the system. During this period, we will reconnect with our egalitarianism as a nation; focus more on a fair and equitable sharing of resources and wealth. There will be an escalating shift towards the left of politics that will be revolutionary. The emergence of far-right extremism in Australia will be put to bed, as Australians will finally see it for what it is i.e., a racist, conservative, and backward thinking ideology that no longer serves any purpose for our great nation.

Other key events that will most likely play out, will be a movement for legalised euthanasia in most states, the legalisation of medicinal cannabis and the likelihood of drug reform in Australia. This will become a major reform for our nation, similar to Portugal or Norway, using a health centred approach. Finally, we will wake up as a nation and start dealing with our alarming drug and alcohol issues and escalate the fight against domestic violence, as a matter of urgency.

The Rise of the Great Southern Land, Outback Mount
Isa, Queensland

The Drug Reform agenda will:

- Spearhead the decriminalisation of recreational drugs.
- Introduce drug testing at rave/music festivals.
- Put an end to the use of sniffer dogs.
- Increase access to free drug rehabilitation treatment.
- Change our perceptions around drug use, not as an addiction but as a disease.

We will not eliminate the black market but it is likely to substantially reduce in its size, free up the court system, and people will be able to seek treatment without discrimination and fear of stigmatisation. Sites such as **www.realmedicine.com.au** will spearhead access for people living with acute and/or chronic pain; seeking the expert advice of practitioners who prescribe medicinal cannabis in consultation with their doctors to help manage their symptoms.

How politics plays out is uncertain, but I think we will see the emergence of new left-leaning political parties. Thanks to our compulsory voting system; a new leader will emerge. This leader will be someone inspiring like Bernie Saunders in the USA, who will be able to inspire the nearly one million Australians under 30 who have never registered to vote. Most people do not realise that funding to the Australian Electoral Commission has been cut, so they have little capacity to follow up on people who have never registered to vote. The Australian Government knows this because if they all turned out to vote, they could change the course of our next election overnight. Our youngest people tend to be more left-leaning by nature. Therefore, it's common sense that they are the future force of change - Our New Hope.

We just need to stop burying our heads in the sand, and I'm optimistic that the counter-revolution and the forces of change will do exactly that. This change will be about building momentum, and we will finally reach a critical mass of people who will accept nothing less than the will of the Australian people for constitutional reform.

The Republic of Australia - January 26th 2023

I envisage that Australia will choose to become a Republic on January 26th 2023. Most people cannot possibly imagine how it could happen so soon.

I am by no means a psychic and let me preface this; my predictions for the future are based on a number of lenses I use to observe patterns with behaviour, ideas generation, energy resonance and mind sets, including: -

- Simply being intuitive and observing and looking for the deeper meaning behind things. It's then just a matter of connecting the dots and seeing patterns.
- Forecasting and scenario planning, one of the tools I use in relation to ideas generation and channelling concepts. I also

test concepts and ideas with others which is another source of validation.
- Energy resonance which is about mapping past, present and future universal energetic influences.
- Using my skill of clairaudience i.e., ability to perceive messages through sounds (music) or words from outside sources, when I'm spiritually connected in one with the Universe.

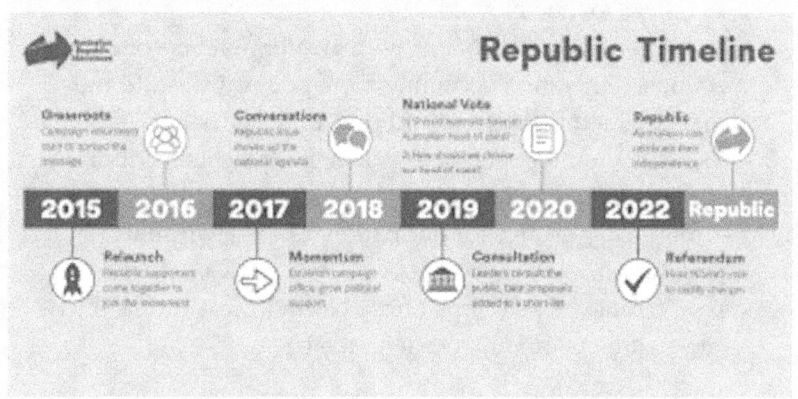

A timeline from the Australian Republican Movement. It is possible!!! This image by no means shows my affiliation with any organisation.

The birth of our modern nation will not only be a product of the counter-revolution, but also a series of events that forces us to determine how our own destiny plays out. This will be a time of great self-determination for our Nation. Likely events include:

- The deep recession that we are destined to have (approx. 2-3 years). This will also be a catalyst for more Australians "Awakening".
- Massive shifts in terms of global financial markets, leading to further instability and unrest in the world.
- Rising right-wing extremism in certain countries, unfortunately including the USA (with the exception of some states like California and New York).
- Most likely with much sadness, the death of the Queen. This

becomes a catalyst for change in itself; with conversations escalating around the debate for Australia becoming a Republic.
- The passing of the media mogul Rupert Murdoch. This will symbolise the loss of his personal grip on our media.
- Extreme climate change events associated with Global Warming and the USA leaving the Paris Accord - this legal process will take four years to complete and would lead to an official exit on Nov. 4, 2020.
- Immense influential change with greater numbers of our younger generation becoming more politically astute and challenging our outdated and prevailing patriarchal systems.
- As more and more people Awaken, this reaches a critical mass of people by 2020-2021, that becomes the catalyst for evolutionary change for our nation. **Change without Revolution.**
- The possible nuclear threat from North Korea and the likely questioning of our alliance with the US.

I fear that Australia will possibly become a nuclear target for North Korea, with a devastating attack being played out. This or some act of similar proportion will be the fundamental shift for Australia (not only the damage it will cause to our environment but on our psyche as a nation). The USA will most likely not come to our aid and possibly, more surprisingly China will. This will only place a greater emphasis on how Australia traverses the US / China relationship, with much diplomacy and care. The only solution for us is to declare neutrality in the world, much like Sweden and Switzerland did in Europe during the 1930s. Do you get a sense of history repeating itself? Most likely!

Sir Henry Parkes envisioned the idea of a Federation of Australian colonies but died in 1899, two years before his dream coming to fruition. In the footsteps of my triple great, grandfather; I see a vision for the birth of a new 21st century Australia, and it's one of the grandest visions one could ever imagine. However, what is central to this vision is the need for constitutional change, when our Indigenous people are proclaimed at the heart of our new constitution. The eventual transcendence of their culture will be the greatest gift to our new nation.

Australia's future holds boundless opportunities, why not walk along the jetty as far as the horizon. See for yourself, imagine the unimaginable!

> **We seek constitutional reforms to empower our people and take a rightful place in our own country. When we have power over our destiny our children will flourish. They will walk in two worlds and their culture will be a gift to their country.**
>
> — Uluru Statement from the Heart

Uluru Statement from the Heart

In the lead up to the looming changes that will occur in 2023/2024, most Australians living and working overseas will see the writing on the wall. I predict over the year leading up to, and soon after Australia becomes a Republic, the Australian diaspora will mostly come home. The Australian diaspora refers to the approximately 1,000,000 Australian citizens (approximately 5% of the population) who today live outside of Australia. Most of these people are based in Europe and Asia and their return home, will help seed and fuel the innovative enterprises our new nation needs; providing an injection of cutting-edge ides, new ways of thinking and working.

Our immigration intake will stay at the same level, if not increase further due to escalating political instability elsewhere and rising public support for embodying our humanitarian spirit as a nation. In addition, our immigration intake over the next six years will see an additional 1,200,000 or more new Australians immigrate here, who will consist of many more enlightened types. Watch our immigration patterns for yourself and see who comes here, you will be surprised. This will also influence our counter-revolution and everything else leading up to Australia becoming a Republic.

Australia will not only birth the world's most modern nation; we will also become a nation that embodies the global force of the future energy to come, that will influence the world over the next 15 years following 2023/2024. Humanity and 2024 will become more about our survival, how we influence the world and the survival of the planet.

In my third book, I plan to write about Australia's future role in the world; a nation with global influence, fulfilling its true purpose and destiny…

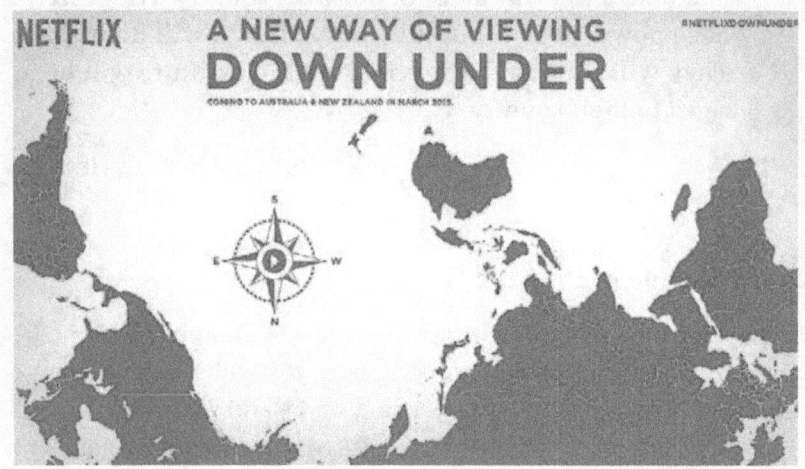

4

CHALLENGES FOR HUMANITY

- DEEPER INSIGHTS INTO THE ISSUES THAT MATTER

> We are just an advanced breed of monkeys on a minor planet of a very average star. But we can understand the Universe. That makes us something very special

> I did my best to notice when the call came down the line. Up to the platform of surrender, I was brought, but I was kind. And sometimes I get nervous when I see an open door. Close your eyes, clear your heart, cut the cord.
>
> Wave goodbye, wish me well, you've gotta let me go. My sign is vital, my hands are cold, and I'm on my knees looking for the answer. Are we human or are we, dancer?
>
> — Human Lyrics, The Killers 2009

The Meaning Lies in Us

The meaning lies in us, and Stephen Hawking knows the science of Cosmology like no other scientist or physicist. He states, "We can understand the Universe. That makes us something very special". But we are at a crucial time in our history, for most of us will experience and witness some of the most significant challenges for our Humanity. In essence, our planet is being forced to evolve. The question in the lyrics asks, are we human or are we, dancer? As Humanity evolves our umbilical cord is finally going to be cut. When this time comes, Humanity will be a dancer set forth on to the Universal stage, however our next performance will be focussed outward rather than inward.

Many of us are already have a feeling that our world is changing dramatically; possibly in a way that we have never seen before. We have grave concerns about our environment, and it's quickening destruction; there remains inequity between men and women, and we have wars that are displacing millions of people but do we care? Where is our humanitarian spirit? We still don't have true equality, with an extreme divide between those that have and those that have nothing. We are preaching about racism and division like no other time, and our political systems are corrupt and divided. They strive to keep people "stupid", and out of desperation people are forced to bury their heads in the sand.

> Meaning doesn't lie in things. Meaning lies in us. When we attach value to things that aren't love – the money, the car, the house, the prestige – we are loving things that can't love us back. We are searching for meaning in the meaningless. Money, of itself, means nothing. Material things, of themselves, mean nothing. It's not that they're bad. It's that they're nothing
>
> — Marianne Williamson

I feel, on the whole; most people would rather not know what is coming and are relieved by their ignorance through the pursuit of greed, security, position, and comfort to dissolve their apathy. But this is nothing to be proud of, a temporary delusion and path of what I call the selfish warrior. Ultimately it's your choice, as there are alternative options. If your awareness is closed, then it's inevitable that you will become vulnerable to the manipulation of others. As our senses become shut down, we end up cowering to others who can control us, and they say everything you want them to say. As a consequence, this then purely feeds your ego nature.

The Challenges for Humanity

The Challenges for Humanity we face are only proportional to our inaction or inability to fight for change. Does that sound depressing? Yes of course it is, but if we all bury our heads in the sand, there will be no one to fight the Challenges for Humanity. There is no time like any other in our human history where world events are escalating to something that is going to result in the possible death and destruction of our planet, but we can intervene! There is a need and urgency for greater activism and community participation in the things that matter. I believe we need some early or possibly radical intervention for our survival, the survival of our planet and Humanity. It just involves getting off our backside, making a pledge and doing something right now!

I believe one of the most significant shifts in our global consciousness is about to take place in the next five to six years. Why this timeframe, I have observed that there are transformational global shifts that always occur approximately every fourteen to fifteen years. Usually, following the initial global event or impact; subtle undercurrents of great transformational change continue through each period.

The next global shift will be revolutionary and powerful in nature; its energy operating from the space of addressing the global inequality that pervades our world. If our actions are mostly focussed towards the "me, me, me" culture without concern for the bigger picture; than the global consequences of the energy shift will be proportional to what is required for us to evolve as a planet. Therefore, the more self-obsessed and selfish we are as individuals (devoid of any meaning) then the more severe the consequences of the next global shift. At the moment, I'm not feeling very confident. In many respects, I believe it's the Universe's way of showing Humanity how we need to change, evolve and transform our consciousness over time. It's so pure and simple.

Wealth Inequality it's pretty depressing! Also, notice there is not one woman among the wealthiest men on earth. As civil-rights activist Dorothy Cotton said, "we are ordinary people, living our lives, and trying…to 'fix what ain't right' in our society".

> Global shifts in our consciousness always involve significant transformational change and power. Humanity must come to realise that the impact of these shifts not only exert a generational influence on individuals but also influences and transcends humankind on a social, political and spiritual level.
>
> Everything we do is about the sum of the interactions of all of us; not only for our planet but also for that of the Universe. As above, as below.
>
> — David Shaun Larsen

Global Shifts over the past 100 years

1914 – 1939

Globally World War I (1914-1919) and Interwar Period. This time was also marked by the Influenza Pandemic of 1918, the spread of psychology and psychoanalysis (attempting to transform our understanding of inherent values) and the Great Depression. The shift in energy also influenced and laid the seed for the Russian and Chinese Civil Wars and a timeline of events throughout the Interwar period and the rise of Hitler, Stalin, Mussolini, and Hirohito.

The underlying theme of these events was challenging Humanity to understand the inherent traditional and territorial values of home, family and nation and our need to protect this at all cost (evident in our nationalism of that time).

1939 – 1956

Globally World War II and culminating in the Korean War - A turbulent time on a massive scale and marked the emergence of the Cold War and ended with major wars such as the Vietnam War. Beginning of the baby boomers (this generation have an intense will, dramatic self-expression, power, and pride) and there was massive immigration during and post World War II.

Over 60 million people were killed, which was about 3% of the 1940 world population, estimated 2.3 billion.[5] Supposedly the war to end all wars. The underlying theme of these events was challenging Humanity to learn about the limitations of conditional love. The ultimate way to experience and develop the maturity of the heart is through grief and loss e.g., death, displacement, war and destruction.

1956 – 1971

Globally this was marked by the time of the Vietnam War, the Civil Rights Movement, and the emerging Counter Culture revolution - This was the time, where our definition of civil rights was revolutionised, dissolved, and transformed. Marked by the height of the cold war, moon landing (connection to Cosmos); the assassination of President JFK and Martin Luther King. It also marked the signing of The Civil Rights Act (1964) and Equal Employment Opportunity. The use of LSD, Cannabis, and worship of the mother goddess emerged.

It was the time of the Counter Culture revolution an anti-establishment phenomenon i.e., the Peace and Flower Power movement (attuning into the higher vibration of service to Humanity). It also saw a massive sea change in our relationship to health and well-being; with a revolutionary emphasis on natural foods, lifestyles, and holistic and naturopathic health practices. Ultimately, this time was attempting to awaken Humanity to our connection with the Cosmos e.g., the significance of the moon landing and realising the damaging effects of war. The Peace movement was the counter-revolution to war and many returned veterans received mixed public support and inadequate long-term health care for conditions such as post traumatic stress, etc.

1971 – 1983

Globally this time was marked by the emergence of two powerful movements for change. The Women's Rights (Liberation) and Gay Rights Movements and the rise of Neoliberalism - these global movements gained momentum. This period was the start of the electronics and digital revolution, height of the sexual revolution, 70s fashion, and disco. Also marked the Iranian Revolution, Pol Pot and his famous killing fields.

The struggle for equality was the predominant theme throughout this decade with many protest marches, and demonstrations and our younger generation were redefining what was rightfully just. This period ended with the emergence of HIV and the publication of "A Neoliberal's Manifesto" in 1983.

1983 – 1995

Globally this time was marked by the fear and discrimination associated with the Impact of HIV and embracement of Neoliberalism - Emergence of the global impact of HIV/AIDS and widespread embracement of neoliberalism. This period ended with the discovery of combination therapy for HIV/AIDS in 1996 which lead to HIV being a long-term chronic illness, as opposed to a death sentence. Since the beginning of the epidemic, more than 70 million people had been infected with HIV and approximately half that number 35 million have died.6

This is more than 1.5 times the number of military war deaths from World War II. Also, this period ended with the genocide in Rwanda which left the world in disbelief (where over 800,000 people were killed in less than 100 days) and the rise of the Taliban as a militia (1994-1996).7

1995 – 2008

Globally this time was marked by the **Global Quest for Knowledge and Rise of the Internet** - This was also the time of many brutalities in the name of religion i.e., the rise of the Taliban as a Government (1994-2007), Sept 11 attacks 2001 and the War on Terror. However, we also saw a substantial economic boom across the world and in essence, this was the start of globalisation i.e., easy borrowing, economic expansion, and technology. Around this time we had much easier travel; access to money and education, that was expanding our horizons and convincing us that anything was possible. *Medicines Sans Frontières* was awarded The Nobel Peace Prize 10th December 1999.

The emergence of the world-wide-web gave us access to information of an unprecedented scale. The Web had broken down previous barriers in many unthinkable ways. In reality, it made our lives unrecognisable by 2008 and when we looked back at this time; we couldn't have imagined in 1995 such change was possible.

2008 – 2023/2024

Globally this time was marked by the **Global Financial Crisis (GFC) and major Global Power-Shifts** - The time which heralded the world financial crisis, thus began a process of global power-shifts and major structural and socio-economic changes. It is a time where Government and especially Corporations rule; the rise of the "nanny state"; loss of rights and civil liberties (including charities) and ongoing major power shifts (some yet unknown).

This has been characterised by the emergence if ISIS; Russia flexing its weight; Brexit (UK leaving the EU) and the election of Donald Trump in 2016 (Corporate CEO). Also, it represents the lifting of nuclear-related sanctions on Iran in 2016; North Korea and its nuclear threats and China positioning itself as the number 1 global economy in 2014. **Australia will become a Republic on 26th January 2023, most likely before 2024.**

2023/24 – 2039

Globally this time will be represented by the hopeful Evolution as opposed to Revolution of our planet. It is often symbolised by a sudden shock event (without warning); with the purpose of bringing the transformational change our planet needs. The chain of events set forth our next Global Shift in Human Consciousness. **See Chapter 10: Humanity and 2023/2024** - *Our Opportunity to Embrace the next Global Shift in our Consciousness.*

The Next Series of Chapters

The next series of chapters relate to my deeper insights around major societal and global issues that are impacting our way of living; ultimately culminating in the next global shift. Understanding the deep threads between these issues is crucial and integral to how we can harness these insights and teachings, for the betterment of individuals and our planet. It's not intended to be an exhaustive list or read, for that matter, but I hope you will get something out of it. Briefly, I will cover: -

- **Gender Equality** - *The Answer to our Evolution*
- **The Environment -** *The Urgency to Protect our Planet*
- **Diversity in Life -** *Acceptance of Cultural Diversity and Universal Sexuality*
- **Humanitarianism** - *Our Global Responsibility for Humanity*
- **Happiness and Wellbeing -** *Our Measure of Social Progress*
- **Humanity and 2023/2024 -** *Our Opportunity to Embrace the next Global Shift*

The Dawn of the Aquarian Age | The Wise Magazine

5

GENDER EQUALITY

- THE ANSWER TO OUR EVOLUTION

> *We've begun to raise daughters more like sons... but few have the courage to raise our sons more like our daughters.*
>
> — GLORIA STEINMAN

> *The beauty of standing up for your rights is others see you standing and stand up as well.*
>
> — CASSANDRA DUFFY

The Search for True Equality

The search for true equality is pivotal at this time in our history, as we still haven't actualised equality for all; especially with a growing divide between those that have and those that have nothing. Therefore, working towards Gender Equality is an absolute necessity and is more than equal representation. It is strongly tied to women's rights and often requires policy changes to achieve the goal of gender equality.[16] According to UNICEF [17] it means,

> *That women and men, and girls and boys, enjoy the same rights, resources, opportunities and protections. It does not require that girls and boys, or women and men, be the same, or that they be treated exactly alike*

On a global scale, achieving gender equality also requires that we work to empower women and work against harmful practices such:

- Female mutilation and sex trafficking.
- Femicide (the intentional killing of females whether women or girls because they are females).
- Dry sex (the act of drying a vagina with herbs, a cultural practice perceived by men as increasing their sexual pleasure).
- Sexual violence.

Women are far less likely to be politically active than men and are far more likely to be poor, uneducated and victims of domestic violence. They have less access to property ownership, training opportunities, accessing credit and gainful employment – many of the things that determine how we socially advance and progress as people and nations.

In many respects, we live in an unjust world, and the forces of change are now opposing it.

Gender Equality is about Balance

> When we live in a world that is very unjust, you have to be a dissident
>
> — NAWAL EL SAADAWI, EGYPTIAN FEMINIST, WRITER, AND PSYCHIATRIST

Lastly, the reduction in the number of deaths associated with HIV since 2010; has been more significant among adult women compared with adult men. Men are more likely to delay starting treatment, less adherent, blunt the preventive effects of treatment, and lead to men accounting for 58% of adult AIDS-related deaths (UNAIDS, 2016).[18] Whether HIV or another disease **men often have poorer health outcomes** in most western societies due to them less likely to seek out healthcare. Therefore, men's health is being addressed with more attention and focussed support.

Striving for Equality is our Evolutionary Intention

Striving for equality is the evolutionary intention that Humanity needs to establish balance and harmony in the world.

The Evolutionary Intention

However, to achieve this, we must first Awaken to our connection with the Cosmos. The Global Shift that occurred in the early 1970s (and energy preceding it) was a significant time for Humanity. Understanding the energy resonance and the counter-revolution (anti-establishment phenomenon) of the 1960's is an important concept. This time was attempting to reconcile and evolve the prevalent belief of devotion to service of others. Given that war was an expression of this energy, the energy shift at that time was trying to connect Humanity to our Mother Earth nature and that of healing.

Ultimately this process was attempting to awaken Humanity to our connection with something much higher; our understanding of the Cosmos, e.g., the significance of the lunar landing for Humanity and realising the damaging effects of war. Many returned veterans suffered major trauma and stress that impacted on their lives for the long haul. They received little public reaction and support when they returned home and access to the long-term health care they needed (such as post-traumatic stress and other conditions). In many respects, this reaction resulted in a distortion within the embodiment of our human spirit, i.e., limited awareness and a lack of empathy and understanding from the public. One can only imagine the profound imbalance and disconnection people experienced caused by patriarchal rule.

The over-arching effect of our Masculinised culture has been counterbalanced throughout time by women effectively, becoming detached in response (often by no choice of their own). In effect, women become drained and trapped by their thinking, appearing to analyse and criticise men. The more over masculinised our culture, then the more extreme the response, such as domestic violence and abuse; whether played out by men or women. In Australia and the USA, the effects of this are possibly our nations' most significant threats. It has helped create some of the highest rates of domestic violence, objectification of women, underlying racism; and alcohol and drug misuse in the western world. In its purity, this is a very straightforward concept to understand without judgment towards men or women.

Suicide is the number one cause of death for men aged 15-44 in Australia, and same-sex attracted Australians have up to 14 times higher rates of attempted suicide than their heterosexual peers.[19] Both Australia and the USA have a poor track record in politics, Australian's (both men and women for that matter) publicly vilified our first female Prime Minister Ms Julia Gillard, and the USA, did the same thing very much to Hilary Clinton who ran for President last year. Although defeated she won the popular vote, go figure!!!

These statistics are not "fake news", and the wounds run deep in our psyche. History always has a way of rewriting events and one day I can only hope we reflect and look back with utter disgust. We have even demoralised our Indigenous community to the brink of despair resulting in suicide rates for Aboriginal and Torres Strait Islander men, doubling that of Non-Indigenous men. I am hopeful that things will change because if it doesn't, it ultimately limits our ability to evolve and mature as a country and rightfully so, become the nation we are meant to become.

We can change this, especially if we start to raise our sons more like daughters and evolve into a Nation with a humble but grand vision for the future. I see this changing with a new form of grassroots political activism that celebrates: -

- Its love of diversity, fairness, and equality;
- Protecting our ecosystems and environment;
- Our amazing humanitarian spirit;
- Our new scientific and technological endeavours;
- Our ability to be innovative, progressive and ahead of its time;
- An efficient and non-discriminatory social safety net, free education and universal healthcare;
- The egalitarian spirit and way of life and being fair and outward looking;
- And reveres all our Elders and has our Indigenous people at the heart of our constitution.

To change this, it's easy, but there is much work ahead of us, and we need the foresight and commitment of people to stand up to adversity. If we look to the Scandinavian societies, they embody true gender equality in the world. History will show that women in the Viking era (circa 800 to 1100 AD) were very much respected as equals, and although the Vikings were brutal, they encountered and influenced many cultures from Afghanistan to Canada. Their ability to be innovative, their curiosity to discover new worlds and travel the high seas, gave them advantage. It wasn't just about rape and pillage (who wasn't brutal at that time) but also a race of people who sought to be heard, to settle, to farm new lands and experiment. Over time they integrated themselves into new cultures and religions. The fusion between pagans and christians.

Norwegian Navy.

Women actively participated in all forms of public life whether as leaders, warriors, medicine/healers, teachers, sacred goddesses and in traditional roles, highly regarded as mothers. Little do most people know, the Viking conquests (which also included women) across Europe and elsewhere wouldn't have been possible without the robust industry of cloth weaving, to weave sails for the Viking ships. The textile industry was a female-led industry and women even as housewives, were seen as business managers, especially in all aspects of the trade.

The Global Gender Gap Report

The Global Gender Gap Report is the evidence base for demonstrating the extremes in Gender Inequality in the world. Gender Inequality is one issue that we can change within a relatively brief period. Being more mindful of Gender Inequality is an important starting point and actively challenging others who perpetrate it no matter what their sex, speaks to our universal compassion and understanding. **Gender equality is the goal**, but it is our practice of being mindful around promoting neutral and equitable ways of thinking that help in achieving the goal. The Global Gender Gap Report[20] measures gender parity or similarity between countries regarding gender gaps in Equality – based on a wide range of indicators such economic participation (income and wage equality); equality in politics, educational attainment; and attainment of health and survival.

However, the human experience is what most counts. As a man who is a pro-feminist, I feel qualified enough to speak about this:

- Being a victim of childhood domestic violence;
- Someone with deep spiritual insight and is proud of their Norwegian heritage (which celebrates gender equality).
- Observations from experiencing cultures across the world, whether my time when working, travelling and living in Africa and the Middle East and elsewhere.

My experience of doing humanitarian work from ages 38 to 42, was a time full of adventure and escapism but it also consolidated many things in my life i.e., being fulfilled with a new sense of liberation and purpose. The events and things I witnessed in life have been challenging on all levels yet so powerful and life-changing. I also knew I was changing as a person, in ways so subtle, regarding my beliefs, cultural perceptions, thinking, optimism and how I saw the world.

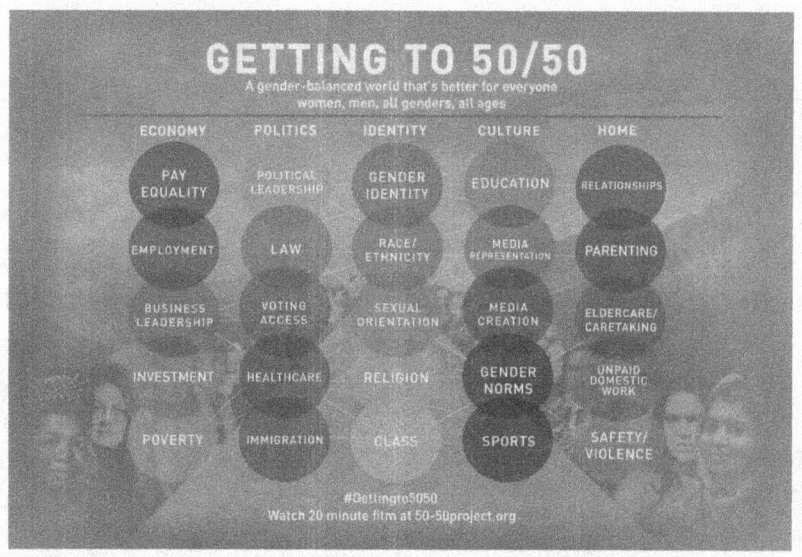

Courtesy of Getting to 50 /50 Let's Create a Fair World for Women and Girls

One of the most significant lessons this experience taught me, was the stark reality that life is vastly different for women depending on where you live. It became bleating evident to me, that those countries which are the most progressive and wealthy, such as the Scandinavian and Northern European countries are near parity regarding gender equality. Whereas those countries who experience some of the most extreme poverty, tribal conflict and inequality in the world such as many African and Middle Eastern countries, women are disempowered. I am quite convinced that there is a correlation between how progressive, happy and evolved your society is with changes in gender equality.

What does the 2016 Global Report reveal?

What does the 2016 Global Report reveal? If we examine the top 10 countries compared to the bottom 10 countries; the top ten are (in # order) #1 Iceland; #2 Finland; #3 Norway; #4 Sweden; #5 Rwanda; #6 Ireland; #7 Philippines; #9 New Zealand and #10 Nicaragua. These countries are far more progressive regarding their political empowerment; attaining educational equality; health and survival between men and women and greater economic participation than Australia and the USA (which sit depressingly low in ranking at 46 and 45 respectively). Also, Switzerland, Germany, South Africa, The Netherlands, France, Latvia, Denmark and the United Kingdom are all in the top #20. The Scandinavian countries and The Netherlands are also happier than Australia and the USA on the World Happiness Report.[21]

The bottom ten countries are #136 Cote d'Ivoire; #137 Morocco; #138; Mali; #139 Iran; #140 Chad; #141 Saudi Arabia; #142 Syria; #143 Pakistan and #144 Yemen. Most of the countries that sit in the bottom 20 countries are mostly from the Middle East and northern Africa.

My theory is that deductions can be made from this data. The higher up you sit in the Global Report, generally the more liberal and progressive the country. It achieves higher rates of gender parity (similarity); educational attainment; higher wealth if nations close their gender gaps; decreased rates of domestic violence, drug and alcohol misuse, and are more environmentally friendly. It's a basic no-brainer, things really need to change in Australia and the USA for that matter because of our poor global ratings in terms of gender equality i.e., compared to other Western societies.

How does this ranking present itself, I call it for what it is, "the Ugly side of Australia".

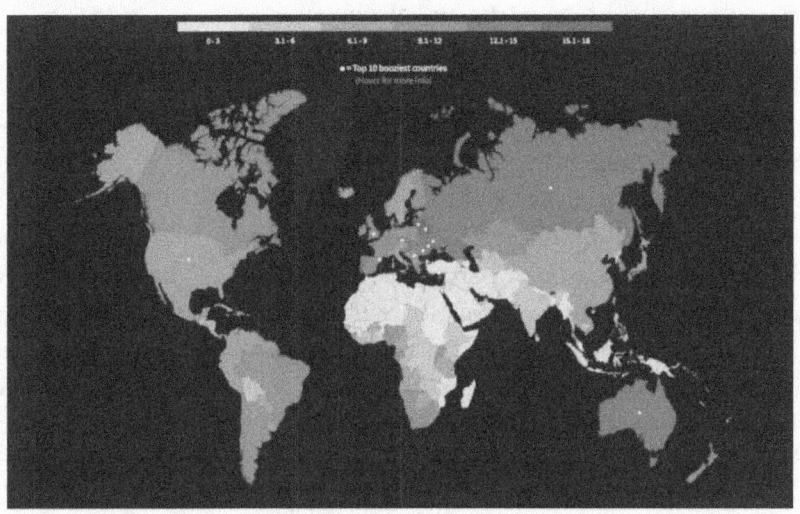

These are the world's drunkest countries - Australia is ranked 10th in the world.

In comparison to other western countries,

- Australia is ranked 10th in the world as one of the most drunkest counties (Vouchercloud compilation of World Health Organisation data 2010-2015);
- Australia has some of the highest rates of domestic violence and related death of women;
- Australia and the USA have ingrained racism at the core of our societies;
- Australians are the world's biggest users of ecstasy, especially among youth (United Nation's 2014 World Drug Report);
- Australia has the highest use of methamphetamine in the English-speaking world or indeed almost any other country (TIME, 2017);

- Male suicide is the number one cause of death in people aged 15-44 (three out of every four suicides in Australia in 2015 were men, and this rate rose to 4 times that of women in the USA).[19]
- There is also clear inequality between same-sex and heterosexual peers in our rates of suicide, acceptance of relationships and drug and alcohol use;
- Australia's "king hit" culture is apathetic.[22]

These statistics are not surprising, especially when Australia rates so poorly in regards to Gender Equality. However, the devastating effects of these statistics are frightful and need to be corrected and corrected urgently; otherwise, our Great Southern land will slip into the depths of despair as a nation that has no heart. Conservative politics and politicians have strangled our country for far too long, with little appetite for change or the willingness to experiment or do anything radical. Data from the Australian Census in 2016 has revealed that the average Australian politician is a white middle-class man, aged 51 with a wife and two children and two or more investment properties.[23]

Our apathy as a nation seems to be counter-intuitive to any desire for change or reform to fix things; therefore, we only have ourselves to blame. As civil-rights activist Dorothy Cotton said,

We are ordinary people, living our lives, and trying…to 'fix what ain't right' in our society.

Hold Heart, the Forces of Change are Occurring

Hold heart, the forces of change are occurring right across our nation. We need to let it happen, as its a form of expression without resistance. The resistance to swinging to the right in our more progressive societies speaks of hope. The resurgence of Women's marches across Australia and the world, are taking on greater significance as a movement for change. The resurgence of Women's marches across Australia and the world, are taking on greater significance as a movement for change.

Two adorable girlfriends Fran Bowron and Steph Sands - both women are making an incredible difference in this World.

Australia is finally attempting to address its high rates of ingrained domestic violence through resourcing community-based organisations and health service projects (we are saying enough is enough). The tireless work of Australian Marriage Equality and other movements to create change for Marriage Equality have finally achieved their goals.[24] The revolutionary Man Up movement is also one bloke's mission to save Aussie men and the creation of Man Sheds that have sprung up across the country.[19,25]

The success of the Hillsong[26] movement as a revolution for change has been a positive thing for Australia and the world because as a movement they embody some of the most anecdotal evidence for achieving gender equality. The success of Hillsong is often ascribed to its ability to bring women on the journey of spiritual development and enlightenment. Maybe this feeds into the reality of our age and what Australia is meant to become a Republic; a nation that truly speaks to equality between men and women at its heart. We need to give credit where it is due, for all these movements for change are genuinely tapping into something that is innate and deep in our spiritual psyche as a nation. Let's Wake up Australia! Far more needs to be done, we need to ensure that:

- Funding to address domestic violence and access to crisis accommodation for women is improved;
- Legal protection for women is drastically improved to give hope for women who have left their partners because of domestic violence;
- The high rates of suicide among men are addressed and support further funding for men's health;
- Our media portrays positive images around the cultural diversity of our nation and our television stops serving mind numbing reality shows that are dumbing us down. Look to Australian film as the answer. Why is it more innovative and unique?
- There is a quota for women in politics given the lack of diversity in Australian politics - it's obvious that men in suits haven't done a better job, given the apathy for our current political system.

Stopping the cycles of Inequality will require a radical change in our thinking and in our political representation. Without this change we will be stuck in the quagmire, of violence, aggression, and guilt; and therefore, we become the perpetrators of such cycles. Is this the legacy we want to leave to our next generation? On the other hand, we can achieve harmonious relationships, if we commit to the principles of truth, justice, and tolerance. The spiritual warriors are those people who aren't afraid to look within, change the way they think, open and heal their hearts and become the wounded healer for others. This kind of healing transformation is what our planet needs right now.

We need to build a critical mass of people who demand change and work towards the creation of a new **Political Movement for the 21st Century** and partner as equals to bring a silent revolution for change. I can sense it; I hope you can?

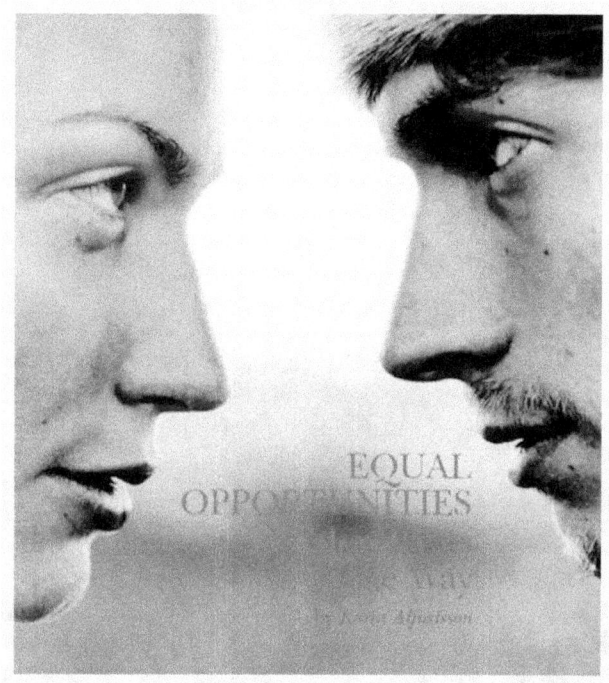

6

THE ENVIRONMENT

- THE URGENCY TO PROTECT OUR PLANET

> *Look deep into nature, and then you will understand everything better*
>
> — Albert Einstein

> *Why do we need to fight our government to protect the environment? The urgency to protect our planet overrides any value of government and corporations. Our most vital legacy is to ensure that our children inherit a world they can live in.*
>
> — David Shaun Larsen

Every Living Thing is Vulnerable

Nearly all species that ever lived are extinct; it's a reminder that every living thing is vulnerable to the fragility of our planet. We might think that we sit at the top of the pecking order but in the Universal scheme of things we are just a blip on the radar. The stark reality is that our time on this planet is precious and how we live and who controls how we live, dictates how we evolve. Therefore, it makes sense if Humanity is to evolve further as a species, any limitation to this; is only bound by the cause and effect of our actions, decisions and that of our collective wisdom today.

Kimberley Ranges, Western Australia.

The virtual control of Government and Corporations is something that I believe demands greater accountability and transparency. They are failing to meet our civil and enduring right to live on this planet. Our society needs to take more civil action around the things that matter, such as understanding the bigger picture to protect the environment. We need to dream big; for our moral protests are barely being heard.

Imagine if there is a global catastrophe or an unimaginable climatic event; the emergency related to this crisis will give us no other choice but to act. In such a scenario, we would need to rise as one and go out into the world, like shooting stars to ensure the survival of Humanity and whatever remaining life we manage to save. We may scoff at such an idea but how do we know it's not impossible? If it eventuates, it is likely to be sudden and happen without notice; in a heartbeat. At that moment, we may wonder why didn't we seize the power of now. The future of our planet is far too important to be left just to our Leaders, Government and Corporations.

Climate Change

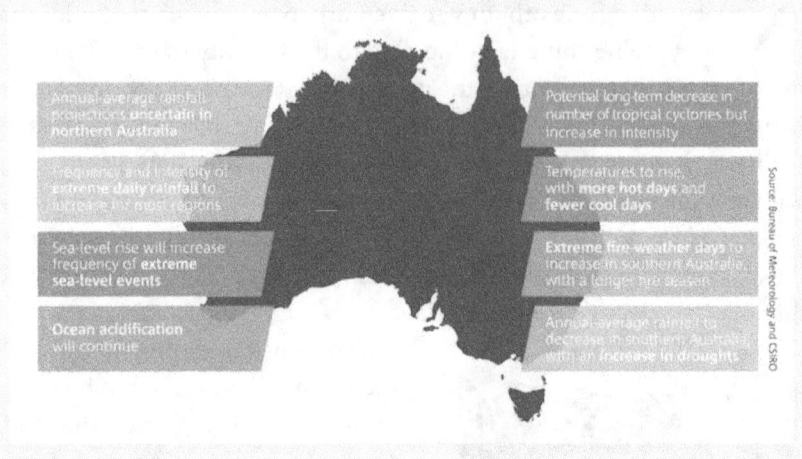

Climate Change is real, and the current state of play is that our planet is teetering on the edge. It is a delicate, self-regulating ecosystem that is gradually becoming destroyed. Climate change is not "fake news", and our handling of the environment will be OUR most important legacy our children will inherit. Humanity has made a profound impact on this delicate ecosystem and our ability to sustain life and our civilisation into the future, as we know it, is untenable i.e., our selfish greed and willingness to conspire to a world of inequity is deplorable. Our footprint is what matters the most, and the most significant travesty facing our planet is our population growth. The select few, who accumulate most of the world's wealth and power, have this needless desire to exhibit their reckless extravagance and greed. They are mostly selfish with no conscious nature or willingness to evolve. However, there are some evolved souls among them who through their philanthropy are changing the lives of others, making a difference in the world and guiding the way.

The issue of climate change has become a paralysing issue for Humanity. The majority of people are either apathetic, ignorant or want us to believe it doesn't exist and will do anything to dispel scientific evidence, keep us in denial and create an environment, to excuse the pun of utter despair. Therefore, most people have become complacent forcing a silent kind of impotence around our ability to act. For those who are starting to wrestle with the big questions and looking for a deeper meaning to life know in their hearts the answers but inadvertently prefer to bury their heads in the sand. They often revert to what they know best i.e., comfort, security and denial. We all need to awaken to the notion of protecting our Environment. If our world's destroyed, we won't be able to rewrite history for there won't be any history to rewrite.

An old water tank at a friend's (Cliff and Andrew) property in Walligan, Hervey Bay.

The Power of Now and Protecting the Environment

The power of now and protecting the environment is imperative! If we are to become dancers and choreograph our next amazing journey through the tiniest eye of the Universe, it can only start and end with the power of now and protecting the environment. It's such a remote possibility, but if we embrace the opportunity to evolve and divert all our energy from war into creating technology to enhance and to protect our environment; we may well witness the ultimate in our potentiality as Humanity i.e., new frontiers, civilisations and worlds we have never encountered before.

Can we deliver such a dream or is it possibly out of our reach? It's not impossible, but it must start today and without question, provide a sustainable world of opportunity for our children. Our Indigenous people knew it; their Dreamtime enabled them to look deep into nature and respect the privilege it afforded for their existence and survival. They lived deep in harmony with nature. Our nations are made up of a smorgasbord of cultures, economies, societies, and people. On the whole, our world isn't very forward thinking, and in many ways, we think with very tunnelled vision; rarely learning from past mistakes and live in a reactionary world often with our issues siloed from one another.

In essence, the superiority of our economic thinking and lack of insightfulness drives our complacency and inability to connect the dots and respond to the issues that matter, such as addressing: -

- Social Justice and Inequality;
- Cultural Divides;
- Humanitarianism and,
- Environmentalism.

We desperately measure the world by values, benefits, and costs; GDP being the centrepiece of our economies and we place barriers around border control and migration with such condemnation. How do we even tolerate ourselves as a Humanity, especially around our negligence towards lessening the suffering of others? Often by no choice of their own; are born or driven into poverty, marginalised by society and are made vulnerable; including our Indigenous people.

Wattle flowers, Kimberley Ranges, Western Australia.

Humankind urgently needs to wake up and develop systems of thinking, operating and viewing the world from an "interconnectedness" between all things. We need to become wiser, creating global systems and visionary ways of doing and seeing things for the greater good of Humanity. It's a no-brainer, and I feel the only way to achieve this is for some global event or situation to raise our consciousness out of the mire that we are faced. The powers to be aren't going to take responsibility and act. Power equals knowledge, and we have "THE POWER and KNOWLEDGE" to change things; for protecting our planet, and the environment underpins everything. Our economies are just "embedded" within our societies, which are "embedded" within our nations and that of the planet. All these systems are interconnected, much like our environment is connected to the sacred essence of life and our spirituality. Therefore, our environment is also conducive to the development and enrichment of our spirituality. Everything by nature is spiritual.

If we are to emerge into the 21st century as the true spiritual warriors of our planet; Tom Hatfield, a British author, states that thinkers such as Raworth, believe measuring environmental performance, will play a much more extensive part compared to the mere financial success of our societies.[27]

> Our carbon, land, nitrogen and water footprints will be part of our own ways of monitoring our personal and national lifestyles, alongside our health and sense of wellbeing
>
> — Kate Raworth, Economist at Oxford University's Environmental Change Institute

Whether from the impact of mining, pollution to climate change, it's no surprise that our societies still place so much value on economic cost benefits versus the intrinsic value of our environmental wealth. We can't pretend anymore that the environment doesn't count, especially if we don't care to count it.

Humanity and 2023/2024 is possibly the next global shift and essentially the crux time for nations, Corporations, and Government. It will be both the end of an era and the beginning of new era. A counter-revolution will emerge in the years preceding this time, as an antidote to the apathy, narcissism, and greed of our current world. A new global emphasis of empathy and compassion will emerge out of the possible chaos and revolution that will unfold. If we are to restore a new world arrangement like no other time in our human history, then there is no time like the present to act. Our current actions if they go unheeded offers a foreboding warning of the world to come.

The Community Conversation

The community conversation in Australia is that we do care about the environment, although we are not always well informed about the detail - people access information, through various media and other news sources. Whenever we hear about environmental issues and proposed solutions for the way forward, many of us seem helpless to know how to act or create the change that is needed. The bleating obvious is that we resonate with it because we truly care about our environment.

A Naked Beach, Kimberley's Western Australia.

Most of us want to leave it up to someone else i.e., other people whom we think are better placed to fix it or have the political power to advocate or work the system. Let's face it; it's easier to have "our heads in the sand" or "sweep it under the carpet". It's the easiest default option. Why would you bother walking the path least travelled, it's a hard slog and bloody hard work? It's easier for us to doubt, think we are not capable or just can't be bothered! This is a lazy response! If you take the time to go within to seek the answers, then in your heart you'll genuinely know or realise that there's an environmental emergency going on. An emergency not dissimilar to our planet having major convulsions and god forbid a massive heart attack. If we don't fix it or defibrillate it right now, we are truly destined to go down the path of no return. This environmental emergency is simply about the death of our planet and life as we know it. Let's not gloss over it anymore; for you have the power to change this right now, nothing more nothing less.

I love to reminisce. In the early days of the HIV/AIDS epidemic in the 1980s; the so-called AIDS victims and community were forced into an impasse. Solutions required drastic force. Hence the formation of Act Up.[28] ActUp is an international direct-action advocacy group working to bring about the end of the loss of lives for people living with HIV through legislative change, medical research and treatment and policies. As painful as this may seem our innate destiny and universal rights to dignity, freedom, and justice include our right to live against corrupt and immoral forces, at whatever time in our human history.

Study history and you will find that there have been many people who have inherently gone against the grain and fought for our human rights. They have all worked to advance the true qualities of our society as we know of it today. Ronald Reagan wasn't perfect as a President and presided over one of the most disastrous administrations in US history. Government inaction led to a battle line drawn between the people versus the government. This inaction was a time where people had to fight for their civil liberties. They also had to challenge some of the most hatred fear and discrimination our planet has possibly ever seen through the global impact of HIV/AIDS.

I have enormous respect for all those people who have fought for injustice in the world and have the utmost respect for their human dignity, at a time of extreme adversity.

The Solution

The solution involves understanding that everything is interconnected, even the conversation about HIV/AIDS and our environment. In some ways, Environmental activism is no different to that of HIV activism. Although both are global issues, there is not the same urgency yet to protect our planet. We either can't see its impact, choose not to or refute the evidence. The protection of our environment deserves a much better, critical response and what we are witnessing is just the tip of the iceberg. If we are going to be complacent, then we deserve nothing but the consequences for our collective actions e.g., if we are to create any significant change, then we need to address our environmental issues right now. It's the most significant issue for our planets' survival, and the only way we can do this is to form a grassroots activist movement to effect change right up to the top, not only for Governments but also Corporations.

Australian Wattle, Kimberley Ranges Western Australia.

Governments essentially are ruled by Corporations and their various sponsors, such as the media and lobbyists. We may choose to gloss over the facts but just look to the most potent example of this in the world i.e., the United States of America (some may say the Divided States of America) and Donald Trump. Trump is just a corporate CEO who is now the President of the most influential country on earth. I'm not sure if this is liberating or brings terror to your soul? Only you can decide. Maybe ask your children or those you can confide in, who will always provide you with the most authentic or truthful answer to your questions.

How Do We Effect Change?

How do we effect change? People power is the only way to affect change, and we need everyone. Join an activist organisation such as Australian Conservation Foundation or GetUp[29], speak out and protest against your elected members of parliament, these are all ways of effecting change. Why GetUp? GetUp is a well-respected grassroots organisation which has a lot of older members and not affiliated with any political party.

> We need to think big for we have no other option than to do this at such an immense scale. We need to think huge billboards, demonstrations, radio ads, and thousands and thousands of phone calls
>
> — GETUP

The most current pressing issue in Australia is the Adani coal mine - the world's biggest coal mine and environmental emergency since the Franklin Dam. If approval goes ahead, the new coal mine and the terminal will ship its coal out through the Great Barrier Reef. The Reef is one of the seven natural wonders of the world and how can we be its custodians if we allow such an envelopment (an enclosing or bad development).

Let's be at Peace with our Environment.

Citizen engagement and people power can have the ability to change this and campaigns such as #StopAdani Challenge[30] can bring that much-needed change. This movement is made up of a diverse group of people, from suburban grassroots activists to traditional owners, farmers and locals directly affected by the mine. The envelopment of Adani has evolved into a situation of blatant corruption, including a billion dollar government handout to flooding of sensitive wetlands with toxic, black coal sludge.[31] Australians have nothing to be proud of if they agree with such an envelopment. It represents nothing but a terrible stain on our great nation - another one of those classic stories of corruption, destruction and criminal history. The company's environmental record overseas is tarnished and with this incident, how can we trust that such an envelopment?

We continue to argue about the effects of Climate Change in a world where we are seeing rises in global temperatures, like no other time in human history. The Great Barrier Reef is experiencing mass coral bleaching, a phenomenon caused by global rises to sea surface temperatures. Scientists certainly don't want to think that our Great Barrier Reef could be in its 'terminal stage'. New aerial surveys have found that two-thirds of our Great Barrier Reef has been hit by severe coral bleaching for the second year in a row.[32] Guess what, we know how to fix it; we just need to stop pollution caused by agriculture, tourism and mining and burning fossil fuels, like coal. We now have a real chance to turn this story around not only for our survival but that of the environment and our planet. It's about the Urgency to Protect our Planet.

BREAKING NEWS

An election has been announced to be held sometime in our future. Hopefully an election for our next President. But like every election how you cast your vote makes a real difference. Citizen or people engagement at every level is critical. We are standing on the precipice for change, and how we remedy this is entirely up to us.

Which side of history do you want to stand on? If you are looking for direction? We only have two choices. Vote for responsible leaders who want to protect our Environment or Vote for those leaders who want to Destroy it.

Many of us feel disillusioned with Australia's two-party-preferred voting system. We must be vigilant like no other time before. Apathy is our worst enemy. Vote for a party that has a vision and wants to renew our economy from the declining industries of the past to one with a vision for our future.

> 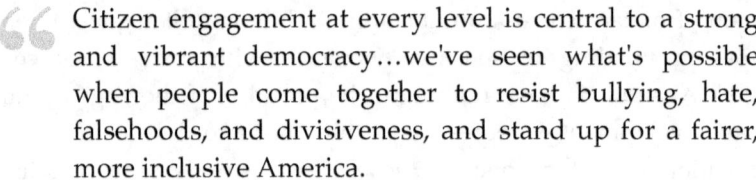 Citizen engagement at every level is central to a strong and vibrant democracy...we've seen what's possible when people come together to resist bullying, hate, falsehoods, and divisiveness, and stand up for a fairer, more inclusive America.
>
> — Hillary Clinton, Onward Together

The Rise of the Great Southern Land

If we look to the forest for inspiration, there is indeed something much more unknown and majestic than us.

7

DIVERSITY IN LIFE
- ACCEPTANCE OF CULTURAL DIVERSITY AND UNIVERSAL SEXUALITY

> For all the Differents among us.
> Live Big.
> Live Bold.
> We need you.
>
> — Gretel Killeen, Author, Award Winning TV Host, Comic, Social/Political Commentator and Zebra.

Australia - One of The Most Successful Multicultural Nations on Earth.

Australia is one of the most successful multicultural nations on Earth. More than seven million migrants have settled here over the past 70 years. It's pretty impressive as a nation, and Australians on the whole; have come to love and respect the cultural diversity of our great nation.

Australia has a solid history of taking immigrants, especially post World War II. We are basically a nation of Differents...

> We should indeed keep calm in the face of difference, and live our lives in a state of inclusion and wonder at the diversity of humanity.
>
> — GEORGE TAKEI

During the decade following the Vietnam War, Australia took more than 80,000 Vietnamese people many of them as refugees or what we call today "boat people". We opened our doors and our hearts and here we are recently voting in a conservative government based on a platform of "stopping the boats". It's quite ironic but sickening as it speaks to our lack of humanitarianism as a nation but not as a people.

This lack of humanitarianism is mostly fuelled by right-wing politicians in either party who promote ignorance and only know how to talk up fear and hate. Are we that stupid, I'd rather not think so but just short-sighted as a nation; as if we don't know any different. People who have Awakened don't hold these views. Fewer than 700 Australians reported Vietnam was their birthplace in the 1971 census, but that number grew to more than 80,000 15 years later.[33]

Bernard Salt, a well-known Australian social commentator, believes Australia can build a case to say that it is the most successful immigrant nation on Earth. He states the global community comprises 195 sovereign nations and if you take into consideration those nations who have a critical mass of ten million or more people; then in Australia's case, the proportion of our population born overseas is 28 per cent: almost seven million out of 24 million Australians. If you add the number of Aussies who have one parent born overseas, that proportion is closer to 40 per cent.[34]

SETTING MIGRATION PACE Top 10 countries				
Countries with more than 10m residents	Foreign-born population (%)	Population 2015	Population born abroad	Population born in country
Saudi Arabia	32	31,540,372	10,092,919	21,447,453
Australia	**28**	**23,968,973**	**6,711,312**	**17,257,661**
Canada	22	35,939,927	7,906,784	28,033,143
Kazakhstan	20	17,625,226	3,525,045	14,100,181
Germany	15	80,688,545	12,103,282	68,585,263
US	14	321,773,631	45,048,308	276,725,323
Britain	13	64,715,810	8,413,055	56,302,755
Spain	13	46,121,699	5,995,821	40,125,878
Belgium	12	11,299,192	1,355,903	9,943,289
France	12	64,395,345	7,727,441	56,667,904

Source: UN

Setting Migration Pace Top 10 countries.

These figures he says,

> Speak to a fundamental truth about the Australian people and nation. There is no other equivalent nation (meaning with a critical mass of population) that has been as generous in absorbing migrants
>
> — Bernard Salt

The only nation with a higher proportion is Saudi Arabia, where 10 million residents out of 32 million, or 32 per cent, were born abroad. But Saudi Arabia's foreign-born residents are guest workers who do not have the same sovereign rights as migrants.[34]

Australia's migrant proportion stands clear of other nations: in Canada, it is 22 per cent; in Germany, 15 per cent; in the US, 14 per cent; in Britain, 13 per cent. Our immigration story hasn't been without fault i.e., not being without ethnic tensions, division or racism. Nevertheless, we need to be proud as a nation, and to its credit, we have managed to do what no other nation has done. We have assimilated (blended into the greater urban mass) a great proportion of people within a short period of time, particularly since post-war Europe and recent economic booms.

When I talk about assimilating cultures, I refer to our ability to gently fuse together cultures, so that we grow with each other. By doing so, we take the best out of every culture and create something that is uniquely Australian, forever changing and subtlety new. Salt states that at the last census, 42 per cent of urban Sydney's population was born overseas. The proportion for New York, the great melting pot, is 29 per cent; for Paris, is 22 per cent; for Berlin, 13 per cent; for Tokyo, 2 per cent, for Shanghai, 1 per cent. **He says Australia stands apart.** Sydney stands apart. **We are different.**

Australia also has one of the highest permanent migration programmes in the world and remains at a ceiling of 190,000 for 2017-2018. The Department of immigration states that this is just over half our annual population growth per annum.[35]

Australia's immigration intake is approx. 14% that of the United States (which is approx.1.38 million in 2015). In literal terms, this means our immigration intake is approximately twice per capita that of the United States. Therefore, per person, Australia takes twice the number of foreign-born people in the USA. Some may say this puts upward pressure on our land and housing prices, especially in our largest cities. This may be true, but the positive benefits in terms of our economy and diversity in our culture far outnumber any negative ones.[36]

Our Most Ideal Path Moving Forward...

Our most ideal path moving forward is celebrating diversity in life!

What are the ideal features that a nation must personify to ensure that sexual and cultural diversity is respected and enshrined in our societies? There are only four things essential for our personal and global well-being. That is equality, civil rights, our freedom, and autonomy.

 The only queer people are those who don't love anybody

— Rita Mae Brown

The brilliant colours of Diversity.

Like Queerness itself, being seen as different by others at various times in our human history has resulted in people being denied their existence, succumbing to atrocious fear and persecution, but also having had fabulous times of celebration, enduring love, unity, and humility. This just means we are forced more than the average person to try and find ways to integrate and orientate ourselves in the world. Much like stealth we try and shield ourselves from the external dissatisfaction and judgement of others.

If you think about it, what has been the most dominant patriarchal force on our planet? Without question, it has been white-middle class men. They haven't had to view the world through a different lens thus taking everything for granted, sometimes with judgement and sometimes with hate. I say this with kindness as I am also such a man, except I'm a man who loves other men. In saying this, I just wish there were more people out there who have the courage to speak from their hearts and aren't ashamed to express anything that is truly meaningful in their lives. In essence, we only create the behaviour and culture we model and therefore deserve.

It makes sense when you think about it, but once we all aspire to true gender equality; we won't view the world through a lens of difference, only a lens of commonality or universality i.e., the quality of involving or being shared by all people or things in the world or in a particular group (Wikipedia, 2017).

Our search for finding meaning in life often leads us back to discovering ourselves. We can bring about change by changing ourselves, and it's never too late. When the Government can create and change laws that govern our personal lives, how we live, who we love, our civil liberties and we are increasingly questioning the integrity of religion; it is imperative that we become more aware of what is sacred and spiritually important to us. Let's all celebrate the Queerness of life itself and stop perpetrating unwarranted, and outdated judgments, values, and beliefs. For we are all created equal, and we must ensure that this is enshrined in our most basic determination to create one global society, for the betterment of Humanity.

Two elephants each with only one tusk, they embody the imperfection of life and the unity, love, wisdom, strength and eternity of a diverse society.

The struggle for LGBTQI human rights

The struggle for LGBTQI (Lesbian, Gay, Bisexual, Transgender, Queer and Intersex) human rights are universal in the world and spans such a degree of acceptance from persecution (as in Chechnya, Uganda and with ISIS) to total freedom, to love openly as in most progressive societies on earth.

At least in 33 of Africa's 55 states, homosexuality is illegal. In Mauritania, Sudan and parts of Nigeria and Somalia, it can be punishable by death.[37] This struggle is essential for our shared Humanity whether you like or not. It's purely about human rights as opposed to the selfless right of right-wing individuals and government to control our destiny which is often based on an extreme religious view.

The Australian Government (including our Prime Minister Malcolm Turnbull) has been totally explicit in this, failing to speak out against atrocities towards LGBTQI people. Countries like Russia and their President Putin, are no better off in their treatment of LGBTQI people and especially their role in Chechnya. They took no interventionist action against the rising tide of brutality where hundreds of "suspected gay people" were rounded up, put in secret prisons, tortured and even killed by thugs i.e., the lowest of low-life men you could imagine. There's nothing manly and by no means, no pride in that, it's just men displaying the ugliest, abusive and evil side of their Humanity.

 Why is it that, as a culture, we are more comfortable seeing two men holding guns than holding hands?

— Author Ernest J. Gaines

Woman Carnavale Rio De Janeiro.

This is offset against a 50-year struggle for LGBTQI rights which started with the Stonewall riots in New York City in 1969. Riots at the Stonewall Inn in Christopher Street, New York, marked the new beginning for homosexual liberation and the struggle for equal rights. Instead of seeking to be recognised according to the norms of the society around them, gays and lesbians fought for liberation and realisation on their own terms. It was the dawning of a struggle that would span a lifetime for most of us but many other people around the world are still struggling today for what is righteous and just. We cannot ignore their plea.

In Australia, the 78'ers were the first group of gay and lesbian people to be arrested for holding a protest march for gay rights in 1978 which then birthed the beginning of the famous Gay and Lesbian Mardi Gras in Sydney. I had the pleasure of working with one of the most authentic and knowledgeable persons in the HIV sector in Australia, a beautiful man named Ian (Ross) Duffin. He works as a part-time Consumer Participation Representative in the former HIV service I used to manage in Sydney. Ross was one of the 78'ers, and we worked in the same building (the former Police Station in Darlinghurst, now a health facility) where he was arrested in 1978. Ross had lived in San Francisco when the HIV/AIDS epidemic hit and was also involved in the early response to HIV in Australia. As humble as he is, Ross has been one of the most inspiring people in my life. Besides being one of the 78'ers, you could best describe Ross as one the most intelligent and articulate men you could ever meet. Ross is a

A photograph of the famous singing Cowboy Times Square, New York City.

researcher, writer, an activist and as an Elder within our community, a beholder of a wealth of stories; a man whose story should be told.

All of us who are openly gay are living and writing the history of our movement. We are no more - and no less - heroic than... Freedom Riders, Stonewall demonstrators, and environmentalists of the 20th century. We are ordinary people, living our lives, and trying as civil-rights activist Dorothy Cotton said, to 'fix what ain't right' in our society.

— SENATOR TAMMY BALDWIN, USA

In saying this, the events of the Stonewall riots and the 78'ers are seen within the context of the modern Gay and Lesbian rights movement, but one of the first Gay organisations was established in Denmark immediately post world war II. LGBT Denmark – *The Danish National Organization for Gay Men, Lesbians, Bisexuals and Transgender persons* was founded in 1948 as the main Danish LGBT rights organisation.

Their aim is to work for gay, lesbian, bisexual and transgendered people's political, social, cultural and workplace equality at every level of society. 1969 after applying for twenty years, they were officially registered as an association, thereby recognised by Authorities. In 1950 it already had close to 15000 members.[38]

We seek to work against discrimination and to function as a dedicated lobby for the purpose of influencing lawmakers, for example in areas such as marriage, adoption, the artificial insemination of lesbians, and rights for transpersons.

— LGBT DENMARK

The Marriage Equality Postal Vote

The Marriage Equality postal vote was a farce! The Australian Government maintained a right-wing view of marriage when most other developed societies on earth moved forward to create constitutional change for equality. It's been totally futile and without excuse; especially when polls have indicated a majority of Australians supported Marriage Equality.

Marriage Equality Movement - it's bizarre that Australia was still debating the issue in late 2017.

The Government proceeded to hold a Marriage Equality postal vote, more as a delay tactic instead of addressing this important civil rights issue. In essence, it no longer became about our right to marry but everything else unrelated to Marriage Equality. In many respects, it turned into a public debate to prove our value and worth in society - our lives, relationships, identity, and worth!

What was most disconcerting is that our Prime Minister presides over the largest LGBTQI community in Australia (Division of Wentworth). Mr. Turnbull had the power to overrule this decision and allow his party to have a conscience vote. The cost of holding this postal vote was an estimated $121 million dollars. This money could have been better spent on addressing poverty, housing affordability, domestic violence or renewable energy. I believe Mr. Turnbull didn't have the courage and dignity to act in the best interests of his constituents.

During this time, I witnessed so many of my gay and lesbian friends (including myself) feel like they had become the victims of something much more sinister e.g. racism, homophobia, denigrating safe schools and same-sex rights to parenthood, raising children and our human rights generally. I even met people who voted No, who claimed afterwards they were frightened or influenced by the NO Campaign. None of these issues had anything to do with Marriage Equality. The Australian Christian Lobby and their supporters were very powerful, well-resourced and funded. Their attacks on social media using an "absolute fear" type advertising campaign, were inaccurate and outdated. The hard-line views held by our Prime Minister's party were actively promoting a potential racial, homophobic and political divide in Australia, like nothing we had ever seen before.

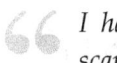

> *I hate the word homophobia. It's not a phobia. You're not scared. You're an asshole*
> Morgan Freeman

What added fuel to the fire, were many Australian churches which were so implicit in this. Their actions were callous and un-Christ-like especially in their support for an extended public campaign. The Christ I know would NEVER have acted in this way. Essentially, the Marriage Equality postal vote, "played out our lives in public". It was a cruel act of negligence that was attempting to set back any idea of social reform in Australia.

Our descendants will hopefully look back on this time with such disbelief and wonder how the world continued to discriminate against homosexuals, created such intolerance for transgender people, people from different cultural backgrounds and even women for that matter! I'd rather know on my death bed (whenever that time comes), I was remembered as someone who has made a difference in this world. If appeasing others for your own political gain makes you sleep better at night, so be it!

The Final Frontier

The final frontier in terms of equality for many LGBTQI people and their supporters was about Marriage Equality. However, I'd like to think that there is so much work yet to be done. The final frontier for all of us, is about how we evolve our human consciousness, focussed on looking outward into the world (not inward) with a sense of greater social and global responsibility.

Some years after I first arrived in Sydney in 1987, I did some voluntary work for the Gay and Lesbian Legal Rights Lobby. I remember researching about gay partnership laws in Norway to develop a survey that could be used to ascertain our community views on this issue at the time. The Lobby was mostly staffed by lawyers, and I think I was one of the few non-lawyers at the time and although it was interesting, it had its own set of politics. I've always felt honoured to be of Norwegian heritage and even more amazed at how progressive they were as a nation when I first visited there some thirty years ago. Even comparing Norway then to Australia now, they seemed to have left us light years behind.

In the 1990's, I remember a friend saying stuff like, "I don't understand why your mob continues to protest", and I'd respond with, "We protest because we don't have equal rights, the same rights as you!". Fast forward thirty years, Australia has made enormous gains in terms of equality. Although this wouldn't have been possible, without the LGBTQI community advocating, marching and fighting to change hundreds of pieces of legislation over the years. This finally culminated in the acknowledgement of same-sex relationships, as part of our De Facto Legislation in 2008.

> The **law** requires that you and your former partner, who may be of the same or opposite sex, had a relationship as a couple living together on a genuine domestic basis
>
> — A DE FACTO RELATIONSHIP AS DEFINED IN SECTION 4AA OF THE FAMILY LAW ACT 1975

The campaign for Marriage Equality drew to an end on Wednesday 15th November. **Justice was finally served with Australians voting for Marriage Equality, 62% for YES and 38% for NO.** The Australian Parliament finally passed the bill as law on Thursday 7th December 2017. It passed with 154 votes in favour and four votes against (after almost 29 hours of debate and 118 speeches). I shared this my moment with mum and realising the reality of this struggle had come to an end; I gave mum a big hug and cried. Thirty years of debating, hoping, marching, protesting and yearning came to an end.

> Is the culmination of our agenda: *the coming together after a struggle.* It captures our aspirations for a fair and truthful relationship with the people of Australia and a better future for our children based on justice and self-determination…*they will walk in two worlds* and their culture will be a *gift to their country.*
>
> — ULURU STATEMENT FROM THE HEART

The passing of Marriage Equality into Law was a defining moment in Australian history. Guess what, nothing has changed; the sky hasn't fallen down and love always prevails over fear. Seeing our Parliament united gave me so much hope, that our great nation can achieve anything.

Let's build on this momentum and start the counter-revolution for change. It may seem impossible to achieve right now, but unity is deservedly much more exciting!

> The beams of golden light are sharp and flickering like

flames, illuminating the darkness of our struggles. Justice is honourable and gives us faith in the unknown. It always speaks to what is constitutionally fair and honest. Our bountiful land offers promise.

Our longing to fix 'what ain't right' in our world inspires so much hope. However, there are new struggles on the horizon. One such endeavour aspires to the exquisiteness of my being and is what is destined and rightful in our beautiful country.

The birth of our new nation and restoration of its soul is now in sight; it's what our self-determination is all about. It's what's rightful and speaks to the traditional owners of our land. It's time to flourish and renew the notion of the Republic of Australia, the great Southern land.

— David Shaun Larsen

Marriage Equality Ambassadors Magda Szubanski, Ian Thorpe and Christine Forster on the Lawns of Parliament House in Canberra today. Picture Kym Smith

 When all Americans are treated as equal, no matter who they are or whom they love, we are all more free

— Barack Obama

The Acceptance of Universal Sexuality

The acceptance of Universal Sexuality is something deeply profound. Being of a Norwegian heritage, I'm so blessed with very few "hang-ups', liberal tolerance, an open mind, sexual liberation and acceptance of diversity.

King Harold of Norway. The Norwegian King gave an amazing speech on love and diversity.

It's something so innate in my DNA it's hard to describe, possibly the closest is how people identify with their Indigenous culture. I am very proud to share the cultural heritage of a land that has a long history of acceptance of gay and lesbian rights. It makes so much sense to me now when I remember my grandfather Vilhelm at the earliest age of 4 would give me a birthday card addressed to "Dear Daisy". It's a nickname my grandparents gave me but for him it was his way of being endearing and soft with his masculinity.

In 2016 the King of Norway in a famous speech to celebrate their cultural diversity said,

 Norway is a place for everyone, regardless of where they come from, their religious beliefs, sexual preferences or even their musical tastes. Norwegians come from the north of the country, from the middle, from the south and all the other regions. Norwegians are also

> immigrants from Afghanistan, Pakistan, Poland, Sweden, Somalia and Syria.
> **Norwegians are girls who love girls, boys who love boys, and boys and girls who love each other.** Norwegians believe in God, Allah, everything and nothing. Norwegians like Grieg, Kygo, Hellbillies and Kari Bremnes. In other words, Norway is you. Norway is us.
>
> — King Harold of Norway

This was said with such proud laughter and cheer from the crowd but left me so sad thinking; imagine our Prime Minister or Governor-General of Australia saying that, it just wouldn't happen here. Hence, what does this say about our country and what it stands for? For me, it says a few things: -

- We are often very complacent as people;
- We are not always concerned about the welfare of those who are more disadvantaged or marginalised as people;
- We tend to feed our apathy or inaction around challenging political, economic, and cultural conditions.
- If we do care, we'd rather wait until the next election cycle to make a passive protest i.e., by then other issues have grabbed our attention.

On the whole, I embrace the U for *Universal Sexuality* (not being defined as anything). Universal sexuality is for anyone who doesn't want to be boxed into a category anymore, it speaks for the Universal sexuality of the 21st Century. Love without judgement.

I truly believe that those people who feed hate truly love nobody and in many ways, I'm so proud of the path I have walked and thankful for it every day. We all seek at some level to make a difference in this world, it's now time we make the effort together, to push ourselves to understand the world at large. It's about our solace and understanding.

Everyone has different ways of finding solace and understanding and as someone who has always felt different, not only in terms of my sexuality but also spiritually; it has always been in my nature to question everything. I may be gay or a man who has sex with men, but sometimes I prefer to be Queer who isn't.

> It is through knowledge and truth that enable us to understand our nature and the world at large. If ignorance is bliss, then who are we to complain about our sad state of affairs. The affairs that decent, commonsense people talk about.
>
> However talk is cheap unless we strive to live meaningful lives, without distraction. If we bury our heads in the sand, it forces us to see nothing but darkness. To only find meaning in nothing.
>
> Nothing but a care for the distractions of life that feed our ego rather than our minds and spirit. As our senses shut down, we end up cowering to others who can control us, and they say everything you want them to say.
>
> It's numbing to the soul. We need to dream big; for our moral protests are barely being heard.
>
> See my friend, if we attempt to understand what is broken both inside us and out; our awareness can expand right to the horizon. But even then, we will not go far! It's only when we see that our wings are also broken, can we understand that we have the capacity to fly.
>
> Through flight, we can soar and soar like angles in full flight. Their flight is our flight and once we truly understand this; we can become dancers on the world stage and possibly choreograph our next amazing journey through the tiniest eye of the Universe.
>
> — David Shaun Larsen

See when we fly, we can start to see many things that others cannot. Come and join me. What I see is a grand vision for this Great Southern

Land. A nation that embraces our diversity; our First Nations people; decent people who are searching for the deeper meaning to their lives and many people or souls with "with eternally deep eyes" striving to make a difference in this world. However we don't always hear of them, over the images and voices of our actors and sports stars. It's not their fault it's ours!

I have a lot hope for change, but it's tenuous. If we are to actualise the notion of self-governance as a Republic, it starts now. At its heart, I have great respect for the **Cultural Diversity of this great land, as it always has and always will be.**

An image shows the Indigenous Multiculturalism of Australia with 250 First People Nations.

8

HUMANITARIANISM
- OUR GLOBAL RESPONSIBILITY FOR HUMANITY

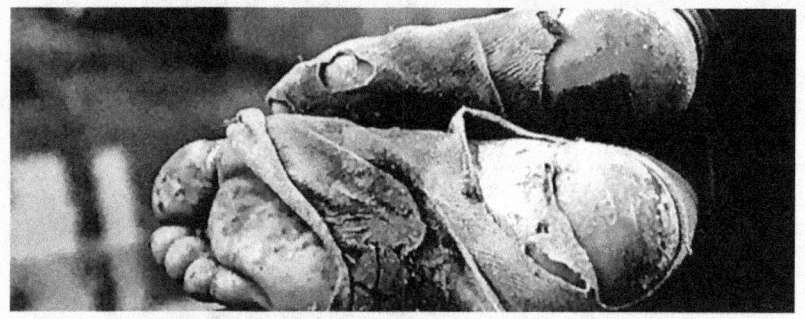

> *Our volunteers and staff live and work among people whose dignity is violated every day. These volunteers choose freely to use their liberty to make the world a more bearable place…One bandage at a time, one suture at a time, one vaccination at a time.*
>
> — James Orbinski, MSF International President, The Nobel Peace Prize speech 10th December 1999

Your Playing Small does not Serve the World

Your playing small does not serve the world and nearly twenty years after this famous Laureate speech was made in Oslo, Norway; we still live in a world that hasn't changed significantly.

Transporting patients from Chisenga to the mainland. Stopped en route at a fishing village to pick up a few sick patients. Although we restrictions on the number of patients we could carry, on occasion we often overloaded the boat.

> Despite grand debates on world order, the act of humanitarianism comes down to one thing: individual human beings reaching out to their counterparts who find themselves in the most difficult circumstances…
>
> And, uniquely for Medicines Sans Frontières,

working in around 80 countries, over 20 of which are in conflict, telling the world what they have seen. All this in the hope that the cycles of violence and destruction will not continue endlessly.

— JAMES ORBINSKI, MSF INTERNATIONAL PRESIDENT

Me thinking about the deeper meaning of life.

For the most part, we still create war and destruction on a scale unfathomable. The Government of the day just finds someone new to blame and to direct their futile need for power and control. Humanity more than ever, at any time in our history, needs to reach out to our fellow human beings who are in crisis. Those people who are experiencing hardship, suffering conflict, and enduring violence at the hands of militia or terrorists. What appears to be something so built into my genetic makeup is the quality of humanitarianism - that part of me that I thought was common to all human beings.

 Life's most persistent and urgent question is, 'What are you doing for others?'

— MARTIN LUTHER KING JR. CIVIL RIGHTS ACTIVIST AND CLERGYMAN

Unfortunately, the older I get; I realise that this isn't so! I feel that there is a humanitarian spectrum aligned with our identity as humans however it indeed mirrors our evolution as people, nothing more and nothing less. The more evolved your consciousness or insight, it is expected that you would aspire to be like a "Bodhisattva" - an enlightened being much like Jesus Christ who has come to the earth plane to alleviate the suffering of others. This is the belief that all human beings deserve respect and dignity and should be treated as such. Therefore, we are all ultimately working towards advancing the well-being and welfare of Humanity as a whole. It's innately in our genetic makeup as human beings; whether you think so or not. Compassion and kindness are critical, but without understanding the world at large, you end up playing small.

 Your playing small does not serve the world. There is nothing enlightened about shrinking so that other people will not feel insecure around you.

— Marianne Williamson

Few Australians realise that Australia along with New Zealand are some of the most humanitarian nations on earth; in terms of volunteers who freely choose to,

 Use their liberty to make the world a more bearable place.

In other words, proportionately we punch above our weight in terms of humanitarian endeavours, if not by the actions of our Government (not abiding international law) but the individual liberty of its citizens. The latter is the story we should be telling our children. It's just that our Government is not as liberated and our society on the whole still chooses to celebrate the endeavours of our actors, media personalities and sports stars than our humanitarians and scientists and other great people advancing the welfare of Humanity.

The UN Human Rights Committee stated in November 2017 that Australia should bring Manus and Nauru refugees to immediate safety. Our mandatory detention policy is inhumane and unlawful and Australia cannot "pick and choose" which international laws it follows[37].

> Australia should end the practice of "offshore processing", immediately close Nauru and Manus Island, and "take all measures necessary to protect the rights of refugees and asylum seekers affected ... ensure their transfer to Australia or their relocation to other appropriate safe countries.
>
> — UN Human Rights Committee 2017

There is nothing enlightened about Australia shrinking on the world stage in terms of its Humanitarian responsibilities.

The Stories That We Should Be Telling

Information courtesy of Conversations with Richard Fidler.

The stories that we should be telling are about people like, Creswell Eastman, who has saved a million brains. Professor Creswell (Cres) Eastman[38] has led projects to abolish Iodine Deficiency Disorders (IDD) throughout the developing world. Children born to mothers deficient in iodine can suffer a range of defects including mental retardation, deafness, speech and physical impairments.

Picture of Crestwell Eastman (ABC RN).

He is an international leader in projects to abolish IDD over the past decades. Cres and his teams have been effective in Malaysia, Laos, Thailand, Vietnam, Indonesia, China, and Tibet. His transformative work with populations in remote areas of China led him to be dubbed, "the man who saved a million brains".

During his first visits to Tibet, Cres discovered that 13 per cent of the population was born with cretinism as the result of iodine deficiency. In the course of his field work in Asia, Cres almost lost his life to altitude sickness. Cres' current focus is on the recurring problem of IDD in Australian and Thai populations. He is concerned that IDD may be affecting the ability of Australian children, and in particular, Indigenous Australian children, to perform at school.

My association with Tibet began in the mid 1980s with visits out to the Tibetan Plateau in Qinghai. But on my first visit there, I had never seen as many people in villages with cretinism anywhere else in the world. So it was a massive problem, in fact it was absolutely overwhelming… It's such a big problem in China because over two-thirds of the population live in rural areas, many of them having to just sustain themselves through what they grow.

In other words, they are born, live and die within a few kilometres… most of the fields, most of the earth and the water are iodine deficient. And it doesn't get in from imported foods or processed foods… So the higher the altitude, the more remote you are, the worse the problem is… If the average IQ of Tibetan children is only 85, and that's what it was before this program started, and people with IQs of 85 can't be educated, they don't really get beyond primary school.

— Eastman Creswell (Cres)

Cres argues that to ignore this problem means turning one's back on the basic human rights of these people and "the most important human right you've got is to realise the intelligence you've inherited from your parents."

Further information:

Cres is a Clinical Professor of Medicine at the University of Sydney Medical School, and Principal of the Sydney Thyroid Clinic at the Westmead Specialist Centre.

To subscribe to the *Conversations* podcast, paste

http://www.abc.net.au/local/podcasts/conversationspodcast.xml into your podcasting application.

The Bridge To Africa

In 1997 I had the opportunity to set up 'The Bridge' Australia's first residential care facility for people with HIV related Cognitive Impairment/Dementia, mental illness and associated conditions. This facility was part of a statewide service administered by Royal Prince Alfred Hospital in Sydney. 'The Bridge' provided long-term residential, rehabilitation and respite care services however the facility relocated to Concord.

The beautiful Victoria Falls in Africa.

I managed the service for five years, and the staff and residents became a part of my family. I have so many fond memories of that time and working there was crucial to my decision to go and do humanitarian work in Africa. It's something that I had always dreamed of doing in life. However, it was my struggle with the ego that deterred me from making a firm decision in my head. That inner voice kept saying things like, "You'll never meet a partner there"; "You'll be away from your family and friends" and "What about your comforts of life, you won't have those in Africa".

It's not that my work in Sydney wasn't meaningful, it just became clear that access to affordable health care was a luxury compared to people living elsewhere. When you compare life here versus somewhere like Africa, you can't close your eyes to the extremes that people face with poverty. It makes you question more and more, what's life all about. Where is the equity in the world? It became innately clear to me that just by our birthright, we have so much opportunity while many others have nothing. I needed at some point to prove to myself that I cared and wanted to do something to change the situation in the world in terms inequity and showing compassion.

In late 2002, the opportunity presented itself to go and work for Médecins Sans Frontières (Doctors Without Borders). MSF is the world's leading independent organisation for medical humanitarian aid and was awarded the Nobel peace prize in 1999. Every day more than 30,000 MSF staff assist people caught in crises around the world.[39] After five glorious years of managing 'The Bridge' I was about to go on the biggest adventure of my life. Africa, here I come...

Out in Africa

All I knew by MSF standards that I was going to what they called "the Hilton project" as they had a speed boat and satellite television which was highly unusual for an MSF project.

The project's base was in a town called Kashikishi, Nchelnge District on Lake Mweru; a vast inland freshwater lake 100km in length that separated Zambia on one side from the Democratic Republic of the Congo on the other. The reason for the speedboat became clear, Zambia had two islands that were on Lake Mweru, Kilwa and

Chisenga islands, as they were responsible for providing HIV health care as part of the broader project remit.

A photograph of a pride of lions I took on my first safari in Africa.

Arriving at Lusaka airport I had no idea what to expect and what was to come, but my first impressions were so memorable; being greeted by a beautiful woman called Clare Nkwanga-Jolly. Clare was our Office Manager among the many other things that she did for the project and the staff, based in Lusaka the capital city of Zambia. She is still a dear friend to this day (limited to the occasional Facebook posts as we follow each other's journeys in life) and her smiling face and warm personality put me immediately at ease, so comforting for a first timer in Africa.

I had so much going on in my head, "I can't believe I'm here", "wow this is Africa", "where I am going to", "it's so hot", "not sure if I should be nervous or excited" so many thoughts. However, what I remembered the most, which stimulated every sense was the joy of just being here - the fresh air and its array of smells, the warmth of the people and the smiling children. It's what I call the rawness of life, and

I now know what people mean when they say Africa just gets under your skin. There's no place like it on earth.

Clare Nkwanga-Jolly.

Never Lonely but Alone

Never lonely but alone, is a state of feeling so integral to my time doing humanitarian work.

Me with a group of volunteers that I trained and worked with, in Nchelenge District, 2004.

Humanitarians aren't some sort of heroes with superhuman gifts. We are just like anyone else, but with a passion and caring to provide a decent standard of living for all mankind and with the realisation, that our destiny is dependent on it.

I have always found this feeling of being alone in the world but never lonely - a classic feature of humanitarians. This was intensified for me when I did my humanitarian work because none of my friends and family could ever really understand what I had experienced or observed. In addition, when you are placed in situations out of your comfort zone, it kind of forces you to grow and to rise to the challenges that it presents or succumb to the fear or inability to go on.

When I worked in the role as a Project Coordinator for Medicines Sans Frontières, it was even more isolating. Imagine not only being the manager but having to live with the people you manage. There was always this time period after work, which I called the debriefing period. This is where I'd be listening to staff offloading their daily woes, usually over an alcoholic beverage. It was like a ritual, by the time we ended up having dinner, I finally felt like one of the team; just like any other expatriate staff. However, there were many days when the going got tough; some nights I'd find myself sobbing or crying to sleep. It was like therapy, as I reflected on the day with no one to talk to. I just had to force myself to sleep and find the strength and resilience to do it all over again. I admire anyone who does these roles for any length of time, for it's not always that easy.

The urge to be a Humanitarian is something quite indescribable. The only analogy I can use actually relates to the intense feeling of depression but exalted in reverse form i.e., the feeling of experiencing immense personal satisfaction and pleasure beyond anything imaginable. I always had a feeling that I needed to do something to alleviate the suffering of others in the world and always will. It's just that the feeling became more intense and stronger as I got older. It's interesting (as an observation), the opportunity to do humanitarian work presented itself soon after I recovered from depression in my mid to late 30s.

I never thought in my wildest dreams that life would lead me down a path of being a humanitarian. As scary as it seemed at the time, the opportunity to eventually work for MSF was like jumping into the void. This new and unknown endeavour would force me out of my comfort zone. Little did I know, I was totally unprepared for the immense freedom, challenges and personal joy this work would offer me in return.

Me in a photograph with a Sub Chief and his delegates in Nchelenge Zambia 2003.

> *In this busy modernized age, it's easy to be blind to the light all around us. You see, there truly are real angels living among us that look just like you and I.*
>
> *If you pay attention, you can spot one because they're quite easy to find. They're the souls with the eternally deep eyes that always act like something is broken inside, but fail to realize it's just their wings.*
>
> — SUSY KASSEM, WRITER, AND FILMMAKER

Wil Groot my brother with a group of children, Willen & Doen Project, South Africa.

9

HAPPINESS AND WELLBEING
- OUR MEASURE OF SOCIAL PROGRESS

> *Happiness is the meaning and the purpose of life, the whole aim and end of human existence.*
>
> — Aristotle

> *Happiness cannot be traveled to, owned, earned, worn or consumed. Happiness is the spiritual experience of living every minute with love, grace, and gratitude.*
>
> — Denis Waitley

How do we define happiness?

How do we define happiness? Well, that's the million-dollar question! I recently went to the world's largest conference on Happiness, called 'Happiness and Its Causes' which is held every year in Sydney Australia. Wow, I'd have to say it's the most amazing conference I've ever been to. I've been to two 'Happiness and Its Causes' conferences, the first conference was over two years ago. 'Happiness and Its Causes' is just so indescribable. It turned out to be the most uplifting and exhilarating conference, especially in terms of the meaningfulness it offers to the participant. It's well worth every cent!

 Happiness is that state of consciousness which proceeds from the achievement of one's values.

— Ayn Rand

Ven. Robina Courtin, Australian-born Buddhist

I have one of the fondest memories of seeing **Ven. Robina Courtin** (an Australian Buddhist nun) at the 2015 conference. The experience helped influence my whole spiritual framework around life. Robina left me spellbound. She has worked with prisoners in the US prison system for 15 years, and even the Dalai Lama never thought that she would become a nun. In 2000, she founded the Liberation Prison Project, a project which works to help transform prisoners' lives, so they may cope with incarceration and deal with the fundamental reasons why they turned to crime.[42]

> Positive states of mind are natural to us. They are at the core of our being. They are what define our mind. They are what we really are
>
> — Ven. Robina Courtin

Little did I know, Robina had given me one of the most amazing insights around my spirituality - even Buddhists can fight for what they believe in because if it comes from the **Right Intention**, then spiritually, it's perfectly fine.

The World Happiness Report

In April, the first *World Happiness Report* was published as the result of a United Nations initiative on happiness and well-being. The Report provides a landmark survey of the state of play around global happiness and also ranks countries by their level of global happiness. Governments, Organisations and Civil society around the globe are increasingly using happiness as a measure of social progress and to assist in policy-making decisions.[43]

The OECD has now committed itself,

> To redefine the growth narrative to put people's well-being at the centre of governments' efforts
>
> — OECD, June 2016

WORLD HAPPINESS REPORT 2017

The first full-day World Happiness meeting was held in February 2017, in the United Arab Emirates. This meeting was part of the World Government Summit. Now on March 20th, we have launched World Happiness Day. A direct summary of *World Happiness Report* is presented below: -

Norway tops the global happiness rankings for 2017. Norway has jumped from 4th place in 2016 to 1st place this year, followed by Denmark, Iceland, and Switzerland in a tightly packed bunch. **All of the top four countries rank highly on all the main factors found to support happiness: caring, freedom, generosity, honesty, health, income and good governance.**

Their averages are so close that small changes can re-order the rankings from year to year. Norway moves to the top of the ranking despite weaker oil prices. It is sometimes said that Norway achieves and maintains its high happiness not because of its oil wealth, but in spite of it. By choosing to produce its oil slowly, and investing the proceeds for the future rather than spending them in the present,

> **Norway has insulated itself from the boom and bust cycle of many other resource-rich economies.** To do this successfully requires high levels of mutual trust, shared purpose, generosity and good governance

These are all factors that help to keep Norway and other top countries where they are in the happiness rankings.

All countries in the top ten also have high values in Six Key Variables, used to explain happiness differences such as:

- Income
- Healthy life expectancy
- Having someone to count on in times of trouble
- Generosity
- Freedom
- Trust

The latter is measured by the absence of corruption in business and government. Here also, there has been some shuffling of ranks among closely grouped countries, with this year's rankings placing Finland in 5th place, followed by the Netherlands, Canada, **New Zealand, and Australia and Sweden tied for the 9th position** (having the same score).

Happiness is both social and personal

This can be seen by comparing the life experiences between the top and bottom ten countries in this year's happiness rankings.

> **This year's report emphasises the importance of the social foundations of happiness**

The Rise of the Great Southern Land

— WORLD HAPPINESS REPORT, SEE CHAPTER 2

There is a gap between the two groups of countries, of which 3/4 of differences are explained by the six variables, 1/2 due to differences in having someone to count on, generosity, a sense of freedom, and freedom from corruption.

The other half of the explained difference is attributed to GDP per capita and healthy life expectancy, both of which, as the report explains, also depend importantly on the social context.

A Microment of Happiness, Berlin 2014

Happiness has fallen in America / The USA is a story of reduced happiness. In 2007 the USA ranked 3rd among the OECD countries; in 2016 it came 19th. The reasons are declining social support and increased support and increased corruption

— WORLD HAPPINESS REPORT, SEE CHAPTER 7

These same factors that explain why the Nordic countries do so much better.

However, 80% of what The Report calls, "variances in happiness across the world" occurs within particular sets of countries. For example in richer countries - the differences are not mainly explained by income inequality, but by differences in mental health, physical health, and personal relationships:

 In richer countries...the biggest single source of misery is mental illness

— World Happiness Report, see Chapter 5

Income differences matter more in poorer countries, but even their mental illness is a major source of misery. Work is also a major factor affecting happiness (see Chapter 6). Unemployment causes a major fall in happiness, and even for those in work the quality of work can cause major variations in happiness.

 People in China are no happier than 25 years ago

— World Happiness Report, see Chapter 3

The *World Happiness Report* chapter on China contrasts the sharply growing per capita income in China over the past 25 years with life evaluations that fell steadily from 1990 till about 2005, recovering since then to about the 1990 levels. They attribute the dropping happiness in the first part of the period to rising unemployment and fraying social safety nets, with recoveries in both since.

 Much of Africa is struggling. It tells a much more diverse story

— World Happiness Report, see Chapter 4

The Africa chapter, tells a much more diverse story, as fits the African reality with its greater number and a vast range of experiences.

But these are often marked by delayed and disappointed hopes for happier lives (see Chapter 4).

Bhutan's Gross National Happiness Index

In 1972 Bhutan's then king Jigme Singye Wangchuck declared gross domestic product was not a meaningful measurement for wellbeing and said the country should instead look at gross national happiness (GNH).

What started as a loose philosophy about how the country should develop became more concrete over the following decades, until 2008 when GNH was formally enshrined in the constitution.

Along with the creation of the GNH Centre and a GNH Index, this philosophy became a formal guiding hand for the government and its policy development.[44]

Learn more at YOUTUBE: Bhutan's former Prime Minister Jigme Thinley explains what GNH means

> We look into the developments through the lenses of society and happiness. We measure the conditions of happiness and we say, OK, if there is increase in the conditions of the people in terms of happiness conditions, then yes, we have developed.
>
> We don't look into technology or infrastructure for that matter as a means to see how we have developed.
>
> — SAAMDU CHETRI, GNH CENTRE'S EXECUTIVE DIRECTOR

The GNH Centre considers four key "pillars": environmental conservation; good governance; sustainable and equitable socio-economic development; and preservation and promotion of culture. It then breaks this down into nine "domains", which are interconnected. The nine GNH domains are:

- Living standards
- Education
- Health

- Environment
- Community vitality
- Time use
- Psychological wellbeing
- Good governance
- Cultural resilience and promotion

Lastly, it conducts research and uses indices to monitor whether there is an improvement in these areas.

My final thoughts on Happiness

Serenity such a beautiful Concert Hall, Sydney Opera House

Happiness is not something that you seek or buy but rather what I call, "a feeling of being content, in flow with life and living in the moment". I believe Happiness is very much connected to one's sense of spirituality - by this, I am not talking about religion. The more you are dedicated to and living on your spiritual path, a greater sense of synchronicity starts to occur in your life. It's not something that we can sustain or prolong, but it's just a state of being that is so indescribable and pure. Often associated with this are Micro-Moments of happiness. These are pure states of happiness and positive emotions that may only last for a second of time, but you experience the awareness and blissfulness of the moment. Micro-Moments of happiness also offer us inner strength, recharge our souls and validate our resilience and ability to become something much greater than the sum of us.

 We are fragile creatures, and it is from this weakness, not despite it, that we discover the possibility of true joy.

— DESMOND TUTU, THE BOOK OF JOY: LASTING HAPPINESS IN A CHANGING WORLD

Happiness awaits! Sunlight Angel Feather: The Angels ask that you feel "happy and optimistic". There are bright days ahead for you!

10

HUMANITY AND 2023/24
- OUR OPPORTUNITY TO EMBRACE THE NEXT GLOBAL SHIFT

> *Humanity is now forced to understand its true nature, challenge its ego and become what it truly deserves to be in the Universal order of things. Forced on our knees looking for the answer, this will be the Global Shift that finally evolves our consciousness.*
>
> *There will be a shock event unlike anything Humanity has experienced before. Out of the chaos, pain and revolution will spur new endeavours, a world of endless opportunity that seeks to drive Humanity to new frontiers, never possibly imagined before.*
>
> — David Shaun Larsen

What About Us?

What about us? At this time in our human history, we are increasingly becoming aware of something much deeper Awakening in us. This is simply about our quest or search for meaning in life, and a fair go for all. Where we have greater control over our destinies, as opposed to the control, greed, and mistrust of Government and Corporations e.g., corruption, unanswered questions and plans that end in disaster.

> Without a global revolution in the sphere of human consciousness, a more humane society will not emerge
>
> — VACLAV HAVEL

This is about our civil liberties and freedoms, giving us greater control over:

- The lives and the decisions that affect us.
- How we care, love and raise our children.
- The health and well-being of the people we love.
- Our right to choose who we love, without discrimination.
- Our right to choose the place and time when we die.
- Our right to indulge in whatever makes us happy without hurting the welfare of others.
- Enabling our Indigenous people to be granted the constitutional recognition and reform which is the right thing to do.
- How the land we love is used; the national parks, the marine sanctuaries and protecting the environment above all else.
- Our right to come to the aid of those misfortunate and **ensure safe passage to this country because we can.**

Are you ready? The next Global Shift will be the most significant for our planet, which will most likely result in a shock event of a scale like no other. It will be the Global Shift to transform humanities consciousness, evolving us into a more humane society. It's going to be our coming of age and a time when Humanity's direction will be focussed towards the future. It will be a future with a global network of communities and a predominant liberal society that is open-minded, progressive and unconventional. Government, Corporations and Financial Institutions will collapse and become a thing of the past, replaced by new Global bodies and systems advancing science, environmentalism, computers and technological endeavours. Things such as green technology, geo-spatial innovation, quantum commuters, digital media, energetic resonance and artificial intelligence will drive this change.

> **We are searchlights, we can see in the dark.** We are rockets, pointed up at the stars. We are billions of beautiful hearts. And you sold us down the river too far…
>
> What about us?…
>
> We are problems that want to be solved. We are children that need to be loved. We were willing, we came when you called. But man you fooled us, enough is enough.
>
> What about us?…

Sticks and stones they may break these bones but then I'll be ready, are you ready? **It's the start of us, waking up, come on.** Are you ready? I'll be ready.
What about us?...
I don't want control, I want to let go. Are you ready? I'll be ready. Cause now it's time to let them know. **We are ready**

— Pink Lyrics - "What About Us?"

Most people whom are "Awakening" or already have "Awakened", instinctively know or feel deep down inside that that some type of change is coming. They're also becoming more aware of their power, sense of truth and justice and true purpose on this earth. Therefore, we need to experience or undergo this immense transformation for the ultimate benefit of Humanity.

The series of shock events will possibly result in a global conflict on a massive scale, environmental destruction, technological revolution (impacting on the planet in a radical way) or germ warfare leading to possible extinction. The people and nations that survive or transform from the initial chaos, will be faced with either two options, the choice to evolve or revolt. How this plays out will be entirely dependent on how resistant we are to change, due to traditional, cultural and societal limitations.

> The world is changeable, and its ability to change is so fragile that a single person can be responsible for it
>
> — A.J. Darkholme, Rise of the Morningstar

Future city: What will Adelaide look like 20 years from now in 2036? Source Sam Kelton, The Advertiser, May 15, 2016

The radical transformation of civilisation

The radical transformation of civilisation, as we know it, will lead to the emergence of:

- A radical change in our political concepts and systems - new movements will emerge appropriate for the 21st Century, based on the individual pursuit of liberty as the primary political value.
- A new global world arrangement, eventually advancing

Humanity to the stage where I believe we will be invited into the self-discovery of other worlds and advanced lifeforms (not the other way around).
- Advances in science and technology on an unprecedented scale; including quantum computers, digital transformation, and artificial intelligence.
- Radical transformation of Disability services such as the emerging NDIS - read on further in this chapter.
- New forms of leadership emerge - change and thought leaders, who are able to inspire and captivate the public with their visionary ideas and new perceptions.
- Greater acceptance of cultural diversity, including "global multiculturalism" and sexual experimentation, diversity and liberty - a movement towards Universal sexuality.
- Communities will advance and merge as intersectional adapters and become more networked. However, communities will be primarily motivated by various ideals, principles and values, adopted at the time ie., our primary way to teach and impart cultural norms & truth.
- A generational shift will be in full force as millennials and Gen X grow older and become more politically astute and herald evolutionary change around the notion of purposeful work.
- Educational systems are likely to transform into a technology-driven world with an array of virtual learning possibilities; with an emphasis on science and social learning, humanitarianism, ideas generation and change management.
- Advances in science will further propel aviation into new realms and herald a new era for space exploration (2030 onwards…). Australia will rapidly develop and transform its Space Industries.
- New technological advances and discoveries in medicine, healing therapies and treatments will emerge, based on complex systems using genetic and energetic resonance for healing (most pharmaceutical medicine will eventually become obsolete by 2034).

- Australia will become a Republic most likely before 2024 and fulfil its destiny to take on a more significant role in the world i.e., the world's most modern nation and Aquarian in identity (January 26th).
- A world of endless opportunity will drive Humanity to new frontiers in Space from 2039 onwards (frontiers never possibly imagined before).
- The global shift from 2039 onwards will be the time Humanity makes the impossible, possible; bound only by our imagination. This will herald an awareness of other civilisations and worlds far advanced than ours.

> If humans are still around after a massive catastrophe, they may look back and think it a grave dereliction that we did not do more to reduce existential risk. But if humanity is gone, and there is nobody left to deplore our era, that doesn't make us any less deplorable.
>
> — Nick Bostrom

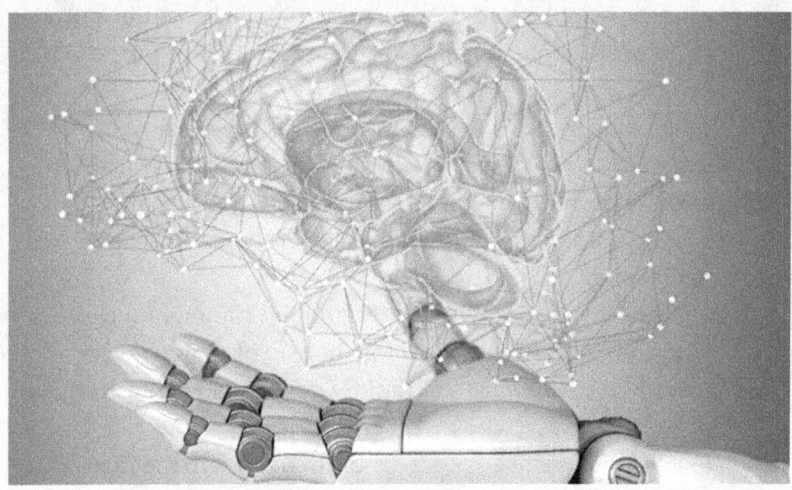

The Power of Cognitive Technologies to Change UX, Businesses and BGO Software. Search by image cognitive technologies

It's also by no design fault that there are many people living today with exceptional purpose, who I believe are destined to create, invent and lead the way through the coming times. IN some sort of way maybe it's the Universe's grand design for helping and supporting Humanity through the changes that are coming. Those who are able to "tune in" to the vibrational shift will adjust, and "ride the wave" into the future. Those who cling on to old ways, patterns, and teachings of the past will increasingly find things "working against them" unless they are open to change altogether.

Australia - A Nation Embracing its Geospatial Future

A map of Australia The Spatial Nation

Despite having a small population relative to its geographic size, Australia punches well above its weight on the global geospatial stage. Niall Conway in his article for GiS Professional provides an impressive overview of the Australian geospatial industry, its active community, as well as the many geospatial initiatives which are taking place in the land Down Under.[45]

Conway highlights the following key features: -

- As a land with a long, rich history of maps. A complex web of migration routes known as Songlines was used by our

Indigenous people for essential seasonal migration. By sharing Songline verses with one another, other tribes would be able to navigate the unfamiliar landscape by reciting the borrowed verses, thereby ensuring their tribe's survival.
- The success of the Australian geospatial industry has been driven by a strong history of investment by industry leaders in order to protect the nation's natural and man-made wealth.
- The Australian geospatial community, together with the space sector, provides direct employment to approximately 100,000 people.
- The country boasts a thriving geospatial community which receives strong support from many local bodies and active representation on a number of international bodies.
- An indication of our country's emerging status on the global geospatial stage was the hosting of an international conference in Sydney this year attracting industry leaders from around the world.
- The geospatial field presents many opportunities; a notable example is Campbell Newman (the former Premier of Queensland) who has focussed his attention on agricultural robotics as an attempt to scale up Australia's attempts to become the 'food bowl' of Asia.
- Nevertheless, the Geospatial industry is not without its challenges. There is a skills shortage; not having enough graduates study surveying, spatial and software development courses.

The National Disability Insurance Scheme (NDIS)

The NDIS is one of the most significant reforms in the health space in Australia since Medicare. Once rolled out it has the potential to be one of the most advanced Disability Schemes in the world and is a clear validation of the Aquarian energy that I believe Australia is embodying as a nation (or Republic) by 2023. For this reason, it is vital that the interface between the NDIS, Health and the broader community becomes better understood.

The Scheme will give people with disability in Australia with real choice and control over their lives. When the scheme is fully implemented in 2019, up to 10% of people with a disability – about 460,000 people are expected to receive a disability support package.[46]

Artificial Intelligence will be revolutionary for People With Ability (Not Disability) - changing lives for the better.

The race for Artificial Intelligence (AI) dominance is fast expanding and will create a significant and powerful shift around how we live. For PWA, I believe it is going to be revolutionary. The possibilities are endless, and even our current sophistication with AI technology is already making an impact on people's lives. An example of this is the AI avatar which is helping people with disability to navigate through technology.

A bold Government foray into AI called the "Nadia Project", aims to help people navigate the NDIS through a virtual assistant. The development process for this project has been co-designed with people with disabilities, community groups, carers, academics, the National Disability Insurance Agency (NDIA) and the Department of Human Services.

AI has the potential to deliver critical services to the public however the "Nadia Project" has been stalled by the Government, amid concern by politicians and the bureaucracy who have been spooked by privacy fears related to the census and 'robo-debt' bungles (The Turnbull government bungle that issued robo-debt recovery notices to 20,000 welfare recipients who were later found to owe less or even nothing).[47]

It doesn't surprise me that such a project has been stalled by the Government. In many respects, this just represents another example where the bureaucratic forces of conservatism and fear are trying to resist the forward-thinking energy that is coming in - radical change spearheaded by science, technology, and innovation. After 5 years of research and development, Nadia is the first commercial project to be launched with this technology. The Government uses excuses that it's early days and there needs to be more testing before it is unleashed on the public.

Sean Fitzgerald, chairman of the NDIA's Digital Innovation Reference Group is a quadriplegic from a bike accident 17 years ago. He said Nadia is a revolutionary program that could transform the lives of tens of thousands of people. He said there were many people with a disability keen to see Nadia enter her limited trial, adding there were thousands of would-be volunteer participants.

> The community is going to start asking more and more questions, and it's time to move on with things
>
> — SEAN FITZGERALD, CHAIRMAN OF THE NDIA'S DIGITAL INNOVATION REFERENCE GROUP

Oscar winner Cate Blanchett is the voice of Nadia, whose face and personality has been created by New Zealand artificial intelligence whiz Mark Sagar. His pioneering work on computer-generated characters for blockbuster movies includes Avatar, King Kong and Spiderman 2.

Cate Blanchett - The Making of Nadia

See it on YOUTUBE: Cate Blanchett - The Making of Nadia

> The more people with disability interact with her, the more she learns...It's all about trying to develop a voice that is positive, forward thinking and optimistic but also cognisant of the hurdles one needs to go through when you're living with disability...
>
> It's a much more democratic, empowering way to deliver a service so that people can just get on with their lives. The liberating potential of this I think is really astonishing.
>
> — Cate Blanchett - The Making of Nadia

The race for Artificial Intelligence (AI) dominance

The race for Artificial Intelligence (AI) dominance is fast expanding. Tech companies are leading the way with companies paying huge salaries for knowledge and expertise, including in academia. This is going to create a significant and powerful shift around how we live; possibly everything from driving cars and providing manual labour (including dangerous jobs) to even cyborg technology and diagnosing an illness without the need for a doctor. China's third-largest technology company Baidu has just announced artificial intelligence as its major focus, including driverless cars.

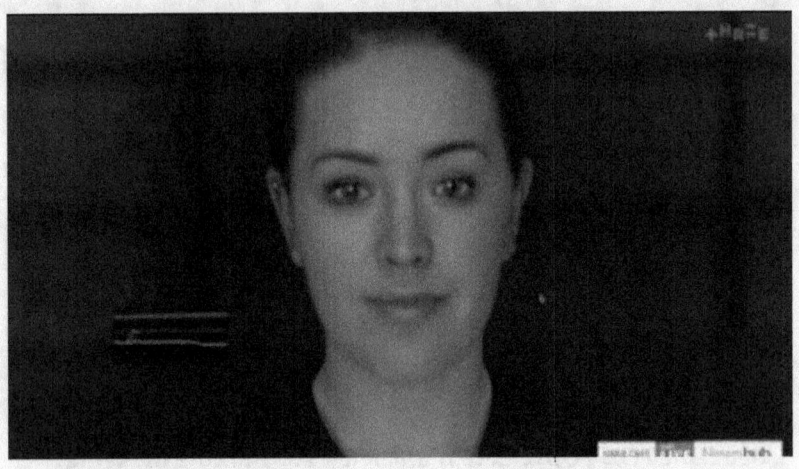

A Youtube picture of "Rachel" - Soul Machines an Artificial Intelligence company, focuses on creating 'emotive' machines and has revealed its first virtual assistant.

Soul Machines (a Kiwi startup) AI company focuses on creating 'emotive' machines and has revealed its first virtual assistant named, "Rachael".[48]

Rachel is an avatar created by two-time Oscar winner Mark Sagar, who worked on the blockbuster movie of the same name. He states that his aim is to make man socialise with the machine, by putting a human face on artificial intelligence.

It potentially opens up a whole new paradigm around how we relate but I ask this one key question, will AI ever possess the ability to feel and possess the innate wisdom of the human soul?

See it on YOUTUBE: Soul Machines' 'Digital Humans'

 So what we are doing with Soul Machines is trying to build the central nervous system for humanising this kind of computer

— MARK SAGAR, SOUL MACHINES

The Rise of the Great Southern Land

View of Australia and Earth as viewed from space.

> In the true heritage of our Aboriginal people, may we pay our respects to the traditional owners of this land, our Elders both past and present who have walked on this most beautiful and sacred earth!
>
> It's not our intention to take anything for granted; your invaluable teachings and seamless actions haven't been in vain. Your suffering and devotion to evolving Humanity has always been in our best interest and always will.
>
> Forgive us, for we do not know any better and have mercy on us, for we are yet to see your divine energy. Humanity now offers you thanks and praise and the realisation and certainty of hope for our future.
>
> — David Shaun Larsen

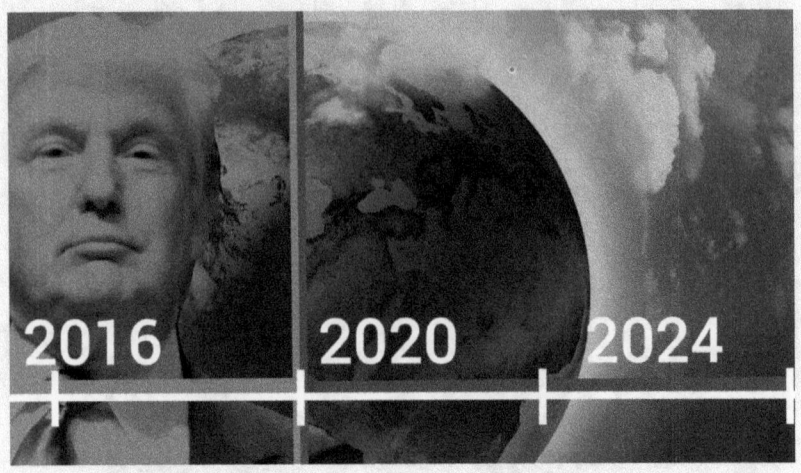

New frontiers, never possibly imagined before.

BIBLIOGRAPHY

1. Wikipedia, 2017. https://en.wikipedia.org/wiki/Kalkadoon. Publication date 10th April 2017. Updated 2nd February, 2017. Accessed 12th July 2017.

2. Chern'ee Sutton, 2017. **Contemporary Aboriginal Art.** http://www.cherneesutton.com.au/index.php?_a=document&doc_id=8. Publication date unknown. Accessed 12 July, 2017.

3. The best single source of information on Aboriginal society is the two-volume Encyclopaedia of Aboriginal Australia, ed. David Horton, Australian Institute of Aboriginal and Torres Strait Islander Studies, Canberra, 1994.

4. Australian Indigenous HealthInfoNet, 2005. **Social Determinants of Indigenous Health.** http://www.coop.com.au/social-determinants-of-indigenous-health/9781741751420. Publication date 2007. Accessed 12 July, 2017.

5. Amnesty International, 2016. **5 Things about indigenous history that you probably didn't learn about in school.** https://www.amnesty.org.au/5-things-about-indigenous-history-you-probably-didnt-learn-in-school/. Publication date 1st July, 2016. Accessed 12 July, 2017.

6. Australian National Museum, 2014. **Collaborating for our Indigenous Rights.** http://indigenousrights.net.au/civil_rights/the_referendum,_1957-67. Publication date unknown. Accessed 10 July, 2017.

7. Sydney Morning Herald, 2010. **Aussie slang? She'll be right, mate.** http://www.smh.com.au/lifestyle/aussie-slang-shell-be-right-

mate-20100125-muaa.html. Publication date 25 January, 2010. Accessed 12 July, 2017.

8. The International Fund for Animal Welfare, 2017. **12 Aug 2017: Paddle out for Whales.** http://ww.whalewatch.com.au/paddle-out-for-whales.html. Publication date unknown. Accessed 11 July, 2017

9. ONWARD TOGETHER, 2017. **ONWARD TOGETHER.** https://www.onwardtogether.org. Publication date 19 January 2017. Accessed 19 April, 2017.

10. Australian Dictionary of Biography, 2017. **Parkes, Sir Henry (1815–1896)** by A. W. Martin. Australian Dictionary of Biography, Australian National University. http://adb.anu.edu.au/biography/parkes-sir-henry-4366. Accessed 18 April, 2017.

11. The best single source of information on Aboriginal society is the two-volume Encyclopaedia of Aboriginal Australia, ed. David Horton, Australian Institute of Aboriginal and Torres Strait Islander Studies, Canberra, 1994.

12. Centennial Trust Parklands, 2017. **7 reasons why Sir Henry Parkes matters.** History and Heritage, Centennial Trust Parklands, http://blog.centennialparklands.com.au/sir-henry-parkes/. Accessed 19 April, 2017.

13. Peter Leyden, 2017. **Why Trump's Inauguration is Not the Beginning of an Era—but the Ends.** https://shift.newco.co/https-medium-com-peteleyden-why-trumps-inauguration-is-not-the-beginning-of-an-era-but-the-end-72a86833f0a3. Publication date 19 January 2017. Accessed 19 April, 2017.

14. Fortune International, 2016. **California Passes France As World's 6th-Largest Economy.** http://fortune.com/2016/06/17/california-france-6th-largest-economy/. Publication date 18 June, 2016. Accessed 11 July, 2017.

15. Investors Business Daily, 2017. **It's Official: Clinton's Popular Vote Win Came Entirely From California.** http://www.investors.com/politics/commentary/its-official-clintons-popular-vote-win-came-entirely-from-california/. Publication date unavailable. Updated 2 July, 2017. Accessed 9 July, 2017.

16. Wikipedia, 2017. **Gender Equality.**

https://en.wikipedia.org/wiki/Gender_equality. Accessed 28 January, 2017.

17. UNICEF, Operational Guidance Overview in Brief, 2017. **PROMOTING GENDER EQUALITY: AN EQUITY-FOCUSED APPROACH TO PROGRAMMING.** https://www.unicef.org/gender/files/Overarching_2Pager_Web.pdf. Accessed February 27, 2017.

18. UNAIDS, 2016. **GLOBAL AIDS UPDATE.** http://www.unaids.org/sites/default/files/media_asset/global-AIDS-update-2016_en.pdf. Accessed 28 February, 2017.

19. Man UP, 2017. **One Bloke's Mission to Save Aussie Men.** http://manup.org.au/the-facts/the-stats/. Accessed 10 March, 2017.

20. World Economic Forum, 2017. **Global Gender Gap Report 2016.** Accessed through the WEF, http://reports.weforum.org/global-gender-gap-report-2016/. Accessed 12 March, 2017.

21. United Nations, 2017. **World Happiness Report 2017**. UN World Happiness Report. http://worldhappiness.report. Accessed 13 March, 2017.

22. Wikipedia, 2017. **King Hit Culture.** https://en.wikipedia.org/wiki/Sucker_punch. Accessed 13 March, 2017.

23. BUZZ FEED News. **The Typical Australian Politician Is A 51-Year-Old White Man Who Owns Two Homes.** https://www.buzzfeed.com/aliceworkman/meet-andrew?utm_term=.eadNn1826#.vjRkYelxo. Accessed 31 March, 2017.

24. Australian Marriage Equality, 2017. **Australian Marriage Equality is a national organisation working to ensure all adult Australians can marry.** http://www.equalitycampaign.org.au. Accessed 14 March, 2017.

25. Wikipedia, 2017, **Men's sheds** or community **sheds.** https://en.wikipedia.org/wiki/Men%27s_shed. Accessed 14 March, 2017.

26. Hillsong. https://hillsong.com/vision/. Accessed 16 March, 2017.

27. BBC, 2017. **What our descendants will deplore about us.** http://www.bbc.com/future/story/20140627-how-our-descendants-

will-hate-us. Tom Hatfield. Publication date unavailable. Updated 2 July, 2017. Accessed July 9, 2017.

28. ActUp, 2017. **AIDS Coalition to Unleash Power.** https://en.wikipedia.org/wiki/ACT_UP Publication date unavailable. Updated 6 July, 2017. Accessed 10 July, 2017

29. GetUp, 2017. **JOIN THE MOVEMENT OF 1,079,803 AUSTRALIANS.** https://www.getup.org.au. Publication date unavailable. Updated 2 July, 2017. Accessed 9 July, 2017.

30. Australian Conservation Foundation, 2017. **Stop Adani's mega polluting coal mine. Take the #StopAdani Challenge.** https://www.acf.org.au/stop_adani?utm_campaign=1707_stpadach2&utm_medium=email&utm_source=auscon. Publication date unavailable. Updated 10 July, 2017. Accessed 10 July, 2017

31. The Guardian, 2017. **Abbot Point coal port spill causes 'massive contamination' of Queensland wetland.** https://www.theguardian.com/business/2017/apr/10/abbot-point-coal-port-spill-causes-massive-contamination-of-queensland-wetland. Publication date 10th April 2017. Updated 10 July, 2017. Accessed 10 July,2017.

32. The Guardian, 2017. **Great Barrier Reef at 'terminal stage': scientists despair at latest coral bleaching data.** https://www.theguardian.com/environment/2017/apr/10/great-barrier-reef-terminal-stage-australia-scientists-despair-latest-coral-bleaching-data. Publication date 10th April 2017. Accessed 10 July, 2017.

33. SBS, 2017. **The Vietnamese refugees who changed white Australia.** http://www.sbs.com.au/news/article/2015/04/14/vietnamese-refugees-who-changed-white-australia. Publication date 14 April, 2015. Accessed 16 June, 2017.

34. The Australian, 2017. **Australia is world's most successful immigrant nation.** http://www.theaustralian.com.au/business/opinion/bernard-salt-demographer/australia-is-worlds-most-successful-immigrant-nation/news-story/1b07d0d672e5eb6ba5e8b6630e5e55af. Publication date 20th March 2017. Accessed 13 June, 2017.

35. SBS, 2017. **2017 - 2018 Skilled migration intake announced.** http://www.sbs.com.au/yourlanguage/hindi/en/article/2017/05/10/2017-2018-skilled-migration-intake-announced. Publication date 10th May, 2017. Accessed 14 June, 2017.

36. Migration Policy Institute, 2017. **Frequently Requested Statistics on Immigrants and Immigration in the United States.** http://www.migrationpolicy.org/article/frequently-requested-statistics-immigrants-and-immigration-united-states. Publication date 8 March, 2017. Accessed 15 June, 2017

37. DW Made for Minds, 2017. **Anti-gay sentiment on the rise in Africa.** http://www.dw.com/en/anti-gay-sentiment-on-the-rise-in-africa/a-19338620. Accessed 27 May, 2017

38. LGBT Denmark, 2017, http://lgbt.dk/english-2/. Publication date 2017. Accessed 7 June, 2017.

39. The Guardian, 2017. **Australia should bring Manus and Nauru refugees to immediate safety, UN says.** https://www.theguardian.com/australia-news/2017/nov/10/australia-should-bring-manus-and-nauru-refugees-to-immediate-safety-un-says?utm_source=esp&utm_medium=Email&utm_campaign=GU+Today+AUS+v1+-+AUS+morning+mail+callout&utm_term=251656&subid=15927438&CMP=ema_632. Publication date 10 November, 2017. Accessed 10 November, 2017.

40. Crestwell Eastman (Cres), 2017. **How Creswell Eastman saved a million brains.** http://www.abc.net.au/local/stories/2015/12/02/4364236.htm. Accessed 25 May, 2017

41. Médecins Sans Frontières. **Doctors Without Borders.** https://www.msf.org.au. Accessed 14 July, 2017.

42. Robina Courtin, 2017. **RobinaCourtin.com.** http://www.robinacourtin.com/. Accessed 12 September, 2017.

43. United Nations, 2017. **World Happiness Report 2017.** UN World Happiness Report. http://worldhappiness.report. Accessed 13 March, 2017.

44. ABC News, 2017. **What happens when a country strives for happiness — at any cost?** http://www.abc.net.au/news/2017-06-

23/bhutan-strives-for-happiness-but-at-what-cost/8633424. Posted 23 June, 2017. Accessed 14 October, 2017.

45. Niall Conway, GiS 2017. **Australia - A Nation Embracing its Geospatial Future.** https://www.gis-professional.com/content/article/australia-a-nation-embracing-its-geospatial-future-2. Published 7 August, 2017. Accessed 28 October, 2017

46. The Conversation, 2016. **Understanding the NDIS: many eligible people with disabilities are likely to miss out.** http://theconversation.com/understanding-the-ndis-many-eligible-people-with-disabilities-are-likely-to-miss-out-61016. Published 7 July, 2016. Accessed 9 October, 2017.

47. **NDIS' virtual assistant Nadia, voiced by Cate Blanchett, stalls after recent census, robo-debt bungles.** http://www.abc.net.au/news/2017-09-21/government-stalls-ndis-virtual-assistant-voiced-by-cate-blanchet/8968074. Published 21 September, 2017. Accessed 27 October, 2017

48. Soul Emotions 2017, **Kiwi startup Soul Machines reveals latest artificial intelligence creation, Rachel.** http://www.newshub.co.nz/home/money/2017/07/kiwi-startup-soul-machines-reveals-latest-artificial-intelligence-creation-rachel.html. Published 9 July, 2017. Accessed 27 October 2017.

ABOUT THE AUTHOR

I like to see myself as someone who has always been ahead of my time and a facilitator of many destinies, which includes being a writer, concept developer, innovator, health professional, healer, and teacher. I am a qualified Registered Nurse and experienced health manager with a Master's in Public Health and Health Administration.

For the past 25 years, my professional career has primarily focused on managing and implementing health and humanitarian projects. This has afforded me with an invaluable insight into the operational and strategic management of quality orientated medical and humanitarian projects; working in a range of challenging and extraordinary situations.

David Shaun Larsen

A writer at heart, and Author of *'Beyond The Black Stump of Eternity'*. I am also someone who is an introvert but has always been a high-achiever with an ambition to create transformational change in the world. Although I value my solitude, having the gift of the gab, enables me to constantly explore opportunities to express my insights and share what I've learned with others. As a healer, I am a trained remedial therapist, spiritual astrologer, and reiki channeler.

Creating the space to have conversations and telling stories that truly matter is powerful. My purpose in life is to improve the quality of people's lives through alleviating the suffering of others. This drives my keen interest and passion in everything; whether from ideas generation to addressing health inequities or writing about a range of social justice and global issues.

What I have realised most about life, is that intention is everything, as long as it is with the right intention! We all have a valuable gift to ensure that those around us thrive because it's ultimately about advancing the welfare of Humanity and making a difference in the world. In saying this, I also provide an exceptional toolkit of services; with a wealth of practical ideas, therapies, and strategies for personal health, wellbeing and empowering others. Whether living a life with exceptional purpose, achieving personal aspiration or striving to reach your full potential; it's important that we work towards the things that matter and are essential for maximising our spiritual fulfilment and success.

Visit me at www.davidshaunlarsen.com
Email: davidsdm@yahoo.com

David Shaun Larsen

A photograph of me at the Honour Awards, Sydney 2016.

PERSONAL AND SOCIAL RESPONSIBILITY

I occasionally volunteer at the Hervey Bay Pet Adoption Centre – just love the work plus the dedicated group of volunteers who work there.

Ideally, I would like to promote the idea of having a writing group for older people in Hervey Bay or elsewhere for that matter.

Encouraging older people to tell their stories is so powerful, especially in this day and age when you can purchase an e-book program such as Vellum (or an equivalent program) for a minimal fee. The power of telling your story, developing your self-esteem as a writer and potentially generating an income source, far exceeds the cost.

Most people have varying abilities to write, therefore I see it as our societal responsibility to encourage our older people to tell their stories; possibly self-publish and become the beholders of their stories.

"Much like Elders do in our Aboriginal culture".

Please note 50% of all proceeds from the sale of my book are donated to: –

- **Doctors Without Borders** (Medicines Sans Frontières)
- **Animal Welfare Organisations on the Fraser City Coast**

www.ingramcontent.com/pod-product-compliance
Lightning Source LLC
Chambersburg PA
CBHW071930290426
44110CB00013B/1548